*COMPUTERS AND
COMMON SENSE*

THE MYTH OF THINKING MACHINES

*COMPUTERS AND
COMMON SENSE*

THE MYTH OF THINKING MACHINES

by Mortimer Taube

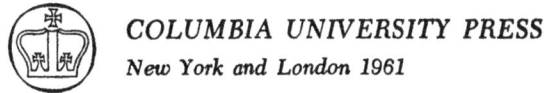

COLUMBIA UNIVERSITY PRESS
New York and London 1961

Copyright © 1961 Columbia University Press
Library of Congress Catalog Card Number: 61-17079
Manufactured in the United States of America

PREFACE

This *enquiry* is an attempt to introduce criticism of science as an enterprise similar in its aims to the established arts of literary, musical, art, and religious criticism. It views the scientific enterprise as an activity carried out by men, not by demigods, nor even high priests. And just as the critics of literature or the arts are sometimes dismissed as sour, uncreative types, and critics of religious doctrine are dismissed as heretics, so the critics of science may expect to be pilloried and what is worse, disregarded.

A critic has two loyalties. He must have a deep devotion to the enterprise he undertakes to criticize, and he must have a sense of public responsibility and a feeling for the public good as a criterion of the significance of special purposes. This does not mean that the critic of science will insist on immediate practical or economic returns from the scientific enterprise. It will be up to him, even more than to the practicing scientist, to insist on the value of scientific knowledge and understanding of the world we live in as a liberalizing and energizing force in the body politic.

So long as science was an individual activity of dedicated men, criticism of science could be considered supererogatory. But in the modern world, science is big business, with its organization men, its dislike of controversy and controversial characters, its share of puffery, and its concerns with plans and budgets, rather than with scientific contribution. Many of our universities, which are supposedly the last citadels of pure and basic research as contrasted with government and business, have set up research institutes and research corporations which aggressively seek contracts and enter into competitive bidding for public moneys.

Ideally, the scientific societies should maintain their own sanctions and exercise their critical duties indirectly through their control of publications, academic preferment, and recognition. And to a large extent they do these things and do them well. But contract research and government grants, together with the opportunity to issue unreviewed reports and participate in symposia, enable impatient and ambitious young scientists to avoid traditional sanctions and the traditional review and criticism of their work by older colleagues. It will be noted that most of the activities criticized in this volume are supported by government contracts and their results have to a great extent been announced in reports and symposia which have not had the benefit of critical review.

It is likely that the present type of grant and contract research will continue to grow at the expense of the traditional cloistered academic research, and it is also likely that the scientific and technical report, especially in new and dramatic technological areas, will more and more tend to become the primary instrument of scientific communication at the expense of the scientific society journal. This means that new types of review and criticism will have to be found. And new types of responsible administrative bodies will have to be developed in the field of science and technology just as they have proved necessary in the field of medicine and health.

Just as war is too important to be left to the generals, and medicine too important to be left to the doctors, so science is too important to be left to the scientists. There is no more reason to expect that science will suffer as it accepts public support in place of endowments from the rich and philanthropic than literature and music suffered when rich patrons were replaced by public support. But public support of science must involve public responsibility and public criticism of science.

A critic will also have his critics. And for their criticism of this work in various stages of its preparation, I am deeply indebted to my friends and colleagues in Documentation Incorporated, especially Mr. Eugene Miller and Mr. Alexander Kreithen. Where I have gone off the deep end, it is because in my missionary zeal I overlooked lifelines which they extended. I am also grateful to Mrs. Carolyn Thomas who was indispensable in the preparation of the manuscript. Finally, like most men, I have a critic at home whose patience and understanding makes all things possible.

But I hasten to add that for all overstatements, understatements, and errors, I alone am to blame.

MORTIMER TAUBE

ACKNOWLEDGMENTS

The author acknowledges with gratitude permission to quote from *Machine Translation of Languages* by William N. Locke and Donald A. Booth (published by John Wiley & Sons, Inc., New York, 1955); *Cybernetics or Control and Communication in the Animal and the Machine* by Norbert Wiener (published by John Wiley & Sons, Inc., New York, 1948); "General and Logical Theory of Automata" by John Von Neuman in *Cerebral Mechanisms in Behavior,* Hixon Symposium, edited by L. A. Jeffress (published by John Wiley & Sons, Inc., New York, 1951); "Inflexible Logic" by Russell Maloney in *The New Yorker,* February 3, 1940; "Goedel's Proof" by Ernest Nagel and James R. Newman in *The World of Mathematics,* vol. 3 (published by Simon & Schuster, Inc., New York, 1956); "Can a Machine Think?" by A. M. Turing in *The World of Mathematics,* vol. 4 (published by Simon & Schuster, Inc., New York, 1956); "Information Theory" by Vittorio Somenzi in *Third London Symposium,* edited by Colin Cherry (published by Academic Press, Inc., London, 1955); *An Enquiry into the Nature of Certain Nineteenth Century Pamphlets* by John Carter and Graham Pollard (published by Constable & Co., Ltd., London, 1934).

CONTENTS

	Preface	v
1	Introduction: Mechanization and Formalization	1
2	Possibility as a Guide to Research Activity	9
3	Mechanical Translation	21
4	Learning-Machines	42
5	The Claims of Linguistic Analysis	53
6	Man-Machine Relations	68
7	Man-Machine Relations in Defense Systems	80
8	Meaning as a Continuum	99
	Addendum: On Scientific Aberrations	118
	References	129

*COMPUTERS AND
COMMON SENSE*

THE MYTH OF THINKING MACHINES

1   INTRODUCTION: MECHANIZATION AND FORMALIZATION

The chapter which now appears as the Addendum, "On Scientific Aberrations" was written first, and it was intended as the first chapter, in order to explain the aims of the book. However, as successive drafts were prepared, it appeared that what began as an introduction became a set of conclusions and evaluations. To keep such material at the head of the volume would be, in effect, to emulate the Red Queen's "sentence first, verdict afterward." Hence, the manuscript was rearranged, leaving room for the introduction you are now reading.

Nothing more is required in this introduction than a brief statement of the scope of the book and the plan which it follows. For a number of years my colleagues and I have been engaged in the development of a mechanized data processing center for scientific and technical information. As we worked to solve problem after problem, as we designed methods for converting raw, formless data into machine-processable form, as again and again we ran into machine limitations, and human inability to formalize intentions and meanings completely, we were dimly aware that outside our own narrow labors, a literature was being developed about new types of machines which would, if they existed, make all our work obsolete. This type of technological obsolescence has occurred before and will occur again. On the other hand, the looms now used in most of our factories to weave cloth are very much like the looms of one hundred years ago, even though anyone who looks at the ponderous shuddering of a loom always feels that there ought to be an easier way, and many inventors have tried to find it. Hence, it seemed reasonable to examine this literature on new machines in the data processing field before throwing away our limited and hard-won gains.

The class of machines described in this literature are supposedly able to translate languages, learn in just the same sense as a human learns, make decisions, and, in short, carry out any intelligent operation that a human being is capable of carrying out. The various chapters of this book examine the evidence for the existence and the possible existence at some future time of such machines.

Sometimes this examination is fairly straightforward and, it is hoped, easy to understand. At other times, however, the argument becomes quite devious and may be hard to follow. We hope that these instances are few and that all cases which occur are justified by the deviousness of the doctrines being examined. After all, if the fox twists and turns, so must the hound.

It will be helpful if we explain here certain terms which are used in the various chapters to indicate opposing points of view or the general nature of the particular issue being examined. There is first the opposition between human and machine, which is sometimes expressed as an opposition between the physiological and the mechanical. It is certainly possible to say that at a deeper philosophical level this opposition disappears. There are mechanistic interpretations of physiology, just as there are idealistic interpretations of physics. But on the level of the special sciences, there are manifold and obvious distinctions between the science of physiology and the science of mechanics and even between physiology and the science of electrical engineering. One of the things implied by the recognition of this distinction is that we will trust the physiologists for answers to physiological questions and electrical engineers for answers about electrical engineering. We will not take on faith a statement made about a physiological question by an electrical engineer, especially one who has no warrant for competence in the field of physiology.

With reference to mathematics, this study recognizes the existence of an opposition between intuitionists such as Luitzen E. J. Brouwer, Jules Henri Poincaré, or Hermann Weyl and formalists such as David Hilbert and his followers. It accepts the view that neither mathematics, nor logic, nor syntax can be completely formalized.[1] On the other hand, it recognizes the enormous value of extending the formal treatment of mathematics, logic, and syntax as far as practicable.

The term "formal," which appears throughout this work, deserves to be domesticated. So long as it remains a private term of the mathematicians it is not possible to understand why there should be limits to what machines can do and what these limits are.

As used by mathematicians, logicians, and computer theorists, the word "formal" is almost synonymous with mechanical. Hence, formal limits, if they exist, are also limits of mechanization. Since this specialized synonymy between "formal" and "mechanical" is not found in the dictionary or in common usage, it will be helpful to explain how this specialized usage developed and why it is the key to the problems discussed in the following chapters.

Consider first the homely example of a suit of clothes made by hand compared with another suit made by machine. We would ordinarily say that the second suit was made by a mechanized process but not that it was made by a formal process. But if the situation is examined more deeply it will be seen that before sewing could be mechanized, it was necessary to formalize it. One tailor may learn from another by imitation; and his skill will be improved by experience as he learns both the idiosyncrasies of cloth and the control of his own instruments and fingers. This learning is not a formal process. On the other hand, before a machine can be made it must be designed, *i.e.*, described, in formal terms. The needles operated by the machine must be strictly controlled and cannot vary with the feel of the cloth or the tiredness of an arm. Furthermore, in the interest of speed certain stitches may have to be simplified and special finishing procedures eliminated. The machine-tailored suit will be cheaper and for most purposes as good as the hand-tailored suit. Only where there are idiosyncrasies in the material itself (*i.e.*, hand-woven cloth) will hand-tailoring be markedly superior to machine-tailoring. This opposition between hand work and machine work is all around us. Hand work may be preferred, not only because of snob appeal but because it is actually better.

Not only some of the work of the hand but also some of the work of the mind can be mechanized, and in the case of mental work the relation between formal and mechanical becomes clearer. If we wish to add or multiply numbers we do so in accordance with certain rules, and whatever can be expressed in a rule can in principle be mechanized. Thus we find adding machines, and even complicated calculating machines, widely used.

There are some mathematical problems which are difficult to understand in terms of rules alone, and the mind finds it useful to use diagrams or drawings to convey the meaning of the rules (*e.g.*, in geometry). So long as diagrams are used the branch of mathematics which uses them is said to be intuitive, rather than formal, or is said to have intuitive elements. In any attempt to mechanize mathematics, the nonformal, *i.e.*, the intuitive elements, indicate a limit to such mechanization. Here the equivalence of formal and mechanical begins to emerge.

Suppose a business man comes to a data processing center with a request for a system to be developed that will give him certain information about his customers. The systems designer and programmer will by a series of questions try to get the client to state his requirements in formal terms. They will say, "If you want to divide your customers between those who live east of the Mississippi and those who live west of the Mississippi, two rules or formal codes will be needed. If there is a requirement for division of customers into states, fifty rules or codes will be needed." The client may wish to divide his customers into different classes of credit risks, and the systems designer may suggest using the rule of frequency of payment, Dun and Bradstreet rating, annual volume of purchases, etc. If the client says that none of these will do and that what he is after is the intentions and moral strength of his customers, the designer may say that these things can't be formalized and hence can't be part of a mechanized data processing system. The client, for such things, will have to rely on his intuitive judgment.

At this point, the designer many fudge a little and offer

to construct for the client a scale of moral strength, say from 1 to 10. Customer A will be assigned moral strength .7; Customer B moral strength 1.6, etc. The designer cannot base this assignment of degree of moral strength on any public fact like "past history of payments," because then the numbers would be measures of such a history and not measures of moral strength. In short, either moral strength must be directly measurable so that it can be replaced by a formal quantity in the system, or it remains an informal matter outside the mechanized system.

It is not always advantageous to substitute formal treatment for intuition, even in mathematics, because sometimes formal analysis involves a great many steps which many times can be safely omitted from proofs and demonstrations. Although *Principia Mathematica* gave an enormous impetus to formal logic, it still contains many intuitive jumps in the course of its three-volume progression towards formal proofs of statements that every schoolboy accepts intuitively without proof. Quine, in his *Mathematical Logic*, was content to present "informal arguments about the existence of formal deductions"[2] because as he puts it, his interest was in formalizing logic and not in formalizing discourse about the formalization of logic.

If the objection to the difficulty of a purely formal treatment of mathematics lay only in its tedium, the advent of the electronic computer would have led to the complete formalization of mathematics. As it was, many problems which had resisted formal treatment because of the number of steps involved became amenable to formal solution with computers. In fact, success in this regard was so striking that many people began to assume that every mathematical problem could be formalized, that is, solved mechanically. This goal, as has been noted above, is not attainable. The formalization of mathematics requires that all mathematical statements be derivable from logical statements; but logical truth itself is informal.

In the following chapters which deal with mechanical translation, machine learning, and linguistic analysis, the resolution of many of the problems discussed will turn on the question of whether language, learning, and thought processes can be formalized; and in all cases the question of mechanization is treated as a problem of formalization. We can mechanize in so far as we can make a formal rule.

It is not always true that formalization, even when possible, is advantageous. Painting, musical composition, and literature produced according to formal rules have definite limitations. We are not even sure that schoolboys should be taught geometry without benefit of constructions.

Finally, it seems clear that language as a system of meaningful symbols spoken or written is not a formal process and cannot be reduced to one without destroying its very nature. That is why historically grammar has been a normative rather than a descriptive science. When language is formalized it ceases to be language and becomes a code. Even those linguists who emphasize the primacy of speech as a physical phenomenon must use the nonformal notion of similarity in order to classify distinct physical events as constituting the *same* phoneme.

Questions concerning the formalization of mathematics, the formalization of linguistic analysis, or the formalization of learning are usually proposed within the context of possibility. Since even the most convinced supporter of formalization or mechanization would admit that none of these ends has yet been achieved, they must be considered, if they are considered at all, as *possibilities*. Hence, we must turn in the next chapter to a look at this most difficult and refractory concept.

2 POSSIBILITY AS A GUIDE TO RESEARCH ACTIVITY

This chapter will be concerned with the use of the term "possibility" in reference to scientific beliefs or research activities; and the use of the notion of possible success as the justification for a research program.

In order to indicate this usage, there can be set down a series of questions involving the term "possible."

(1) Is it possible to translate by machine from one language to another?
(2) Is it possible to build a perpetual motion machine?
(3) Is it possible to measure exactly the position and velocity of an electron?
(4) Is it possible to see God?
(5) Is it possible to have extrasensory perception?
(6) Is it possible to increase our understanding of the nature of combustion?
(7) Is it possible to set up a platform in space?
(8) Is it possible that the combined proposition "p and not p" is true?
(9) Is it possible to prove that the set of axioms of arithmetic is both complete and consistent?
(10) Is it possible for a machine to think?

It will be seen from a study of the above questions that

some of them will ordinarily be answered with an immediate "yes," some with an immediate "no," and some will elicit an equivocal "maybe." It is also true that it would be a comparatively easy matter to get agreement on some of the questions, but others would occasion much disagreement which, perhaps, could only be resolved by a thorough analysis, not only of the meaning of "possible," but of the other substantive words in the question. For example, "p and not p" is a contradiction. Therefore, one can deny the possibility of (8) with complete assurance that the progress of science will never prove him wrong. A research program to ascertain the possibility of (8) would be nonsense.

Concerning (6) the answer is an unequivocal "yes." Combustion is a natural phenomenon which over the past century and a half has been better and better understood as a result of constant study. Hence, it is entirely reasonable or possible to increase our knowledge of combustion by continuing to study it. A research program devoted to increasing our understanding of the nature of combustion would require no justification other than the determination of the competence of the investigators.

Estimating the answer to (7) is a little more difficult. In view of present accomplishments in rocketry and satellites, it certainly is reasonable to suppose that increased knowledge of propulsion, guidance, and shielding, all of which have the same character as increased knowledge of combustion, makes the answer to (7) "yes." We may never succeed in getting a platform into space. On the other hand, by extrapolation from present activities it is certainly possible and its achievement is a reasonable goal of research; assuming that there is some utility for science in general, for communications, or defense, in getting a platform into space.

Possibility as a Guide 11

Although every year the Patent Office receives numerous applications for patents on perpetual motion machines, most people with any scientific sophistication would say that the answer to (2) is an unequivocal "no." It should be noted, however, that whereas (8) is contradictory in itself, there is nothing contradictory about (2) and hence the impossibility of (2); or the negative answer must follow not from (2) itself but from other statements which are generally believed and from which the impossibility of (2) can be derived. For example, if one accepts the second law of thermodynamics as true, then the answer to (2) is "no." If someone wished to engage in research on (2) it would be reasonable to ask him first to consider the second law of thermodynamics. It would not be reasonable to accept as unquestionably true the second law of thermodynamics and also to support research on (2).

Question (3) represents a similar problem, although the opposition between (3) and any particular law of physics is not as clear as the opposition between (2) and the second law of thermodynamics. It can be said that if the Heisenberg principle of indeterminism is true, the answer to (3) is "no," but some people with an itch to be determinists have attempted to argue that the Heisenberg principle sets up only a practical difficulty to the measurement of the exact position and velocity of an electron and that it is reasonable to suppose that someday these practical difficulties will be overcome so that the answer to (3) is, therefore, "yes." Nevertheless, most members of the scientific community would answer (3) with "no," and it is not likely that a proposal for research to measure the exact position and velocity of an electron would gain much support at this time. It should be noted, however, that in the case of (3) a difference of opinion may center around a different interpretation of the meaning of "possible." The question of interpretation of "possible" did not occur in the cases of questions (2), (6), (7), and (8), largely because the answers to the questions seemed to be unequivocal and certain.

Question (4) is the kind of question which really gives trouble because there are some people who would answer this question with an unequivocal "yes" and there are others who would answer it with an unequivocal "no." In this circumstance, both the group which said "yes" and the group which said "no" would defend their positions by offering various interpretations of the question itself. For example, those who said "no" might argue as follows: (a) God is incorporeal; (b) God has no color; (c) God does not reflect light; (d) the eye can only see color as reflected by light from corporeal bodies; therefore, it is not possible to see God. Those who would answer (4) with "yes" would say God is present in all His works. Although the eyes are involved with seeing, they are involved only as a stimulus of a certain kind and do not themselves determine what is seen. It is the soul which sees, and for the soul to see God means only that God is present to the soul and therefore it is possible to see God. It will be seen that the question is now much expanded. It cannot be answered unequivocally without investigations into the nature of seeing, color, corporeality, the soul, etc. Even though the question is thus enlarged and seems to involve the prior answer to a number of other most difficult questions, I think it would be discovered that those who answered "no" would be impatient of such investigations, whereas those who answered "yes" would also be impatient. In fact, it might be said that the answer to (4) is determined by an attitude of mind which is not modifiable by any results of scientific research. Hence, both the group which answered "yes" and the group which answered "no" would agree that it is not reasonable to have a scientific research project to determine the answer to (4).

Question (5) is similar to (4) in that one would probably discover heated opinions on both sides; that is, there would be loud and indignant "no's" and similarly loud and positive "yes's." But (5) differs from (4) in that at least some people have advocated and carried out research programs to find out whether the answer is "yes" or "no." But those who are certain that the answer is "no" would condemn such research programs as wasteful of money and scientific energy. They might argue in two ways: They might say that perception is by definition sensory and therefore (5) reduces to (8), is contradictory, and can be answered "no" without any research programs. Those who answered "yes" or believed in research programs to determine the possibility of extrasensory perception would reject the definition of perception as sensory and give examples of perception which seemed unmediated by sensory stimulation. Their research programs would be an attempt to find warranted and unequivocal instances of perception unmediated by sensory stimulation.

Up until 1931 many mathematicians would have answered question (9) with an unequivocal "yes"; but in 1931 there appeared Kurt Goedel's important study, *Ueber formal unentscheidbare Saetze der Principia Mathematica und verwandter Systeme* ("On Formally Undecidable Propositions of Principia Mathematica and Related Systems"), which proved that the answer to (9) is "no." This answer has relevance not only to formal logic and mathematics, but to statements of the possibilities for machines. For example, Turing, who answered (10) with "yes," nevertheless recognized that

14 Possibility as a Guide

the most serious limitations concerning what computers can or cannot do follows from Goedel's proof: "There are a number of results of mathematical logic which can be used to show that there are limitations to the powers of discrete-state machines. The best known of these results is known as Goedel's theorem. . . ."[1] A similar conclusion was drawn by Nagel and Newman:

> Goedel's conclusions also have a bearing on the question whether calculating machines can be constructed which would be substitutes for a living mathematical intelligence. Such machines, as currently constructed and planned, operate in obedience to a fixed set of directives built in, and they involve mechanisms which proceed in a step-by-step manner. But in the light of Goedel's incompleteness theorem, there is an endless set of problems in elementary number theory for which such machines are inherently incapable of supplying answers, however complex their built-in mechanisms may be and however rapid their operations. It may very well be the case that the human brain is itself a "machine" with built-in limitations of its own, and that there are mathematical problems which it is incapable of solving. Even so, the human brain appears to embody a structure of rules of operation which is far more powerful than the structure of currently conceived artificial machines. There is no immediate prospect of replacing the human mind by robots.[2]

Thus there seems to be established a relationship between questions (9) and (10): that if the answer to (9) is "no," the answer to (10) is "no." Nevertheless, it must be recognized that this relationship is usually overlooked. Even Turing, who certainly recognized the relationship, as indicated above, concluded that the answer to (10) is "yes." However, Turing felt that the question as presented in (10) is basically meaningless and should be restated in some such fashion as the following: "Is it possible for machines to do what humans do when humans do what is called thinking?" In his paper

Possibility as a Guide 15

"Can a Machine Think?" Turing substitutes for this direct question a question concerning the ability of machines to play a certain kind of game which presumably involves intelligence and would involve the use of thought if played by human beings. Turing's conclusions in this matter are most interesting, because he considers not only the possibility of machines doing what would be called "thinking" if done by a human being, but also the value of conjectures of this sort to provide programs of research:

> It will simplify matters for the reader if I explain first my own beliefs in the matter. Consider first the more accurate form of the question. I believe that in about fifty years' time it will be possible to programme computers, with a storage capacity of about 10^9, to make them play the imitation game so well that an average interrogator will not have more than 70 per cent. chance of making the right identification after five minutes of questioning. The original question, "Can machines think?" I believe to be too meaningless to deserve discussion. Nevertheless I believe that at the end of the century the use of words and general educated opinion will have altered so much that one will be able to speak of machines thinking without expecting to be contradicted. I believe further that no useful purpose is served by concealing these beliefs. The popular view that scientists proceed inexorably from well-established fact to well-established fact, never being influenced by any unproved conjecture, is quite mistaken. Provided it is made clear which are proved facts and which are conjectures, no harm can result. Conjectures are of great importance since they suggest useful lines of research.[3]

By emphasizing the role of conjecture and belief as valuable in suggesting lines of research, Turing discloses another ambiguity which invests the notion of possibility, namely, its reference to a belief that the *future* answer will be "yes." One may believe that something is possible now without

16   Possibility as a Guide

having any feeling one way or the other concerning the outcome of future events. For example, one might say: "It is possible that the number of shingles on a house is a prime number," without any strong feelings one way or the other. And this possibility would remain until the shingles were counted, at which time the possibility would disappear and it would become certain that the number of shingles was a prime number or was not a prime number. It may be said that the state of the roof doesn't change by the act of counting, and this is certainly the case. But belief changes from a state of suspension (possibility) to a state of certainty. There seems some relationship here to Turing's belief in what will happen fifty years hence. But there is also a most important difference between the example presented here and belief or conjecture as a guide to research. It is not likely that anyone would seriously propose counting shingles on housetops as a research project to determine which collections of shingles were denoted by prime numbers. But if someone advocated research on the development of thinking machines based on the conjecture or belief in their possibility, he would certainly mean that, although there was no absolute guarantee of a successful outcome, there were strong reasons to predict success. In other words, bare logical possibility is not a valid belief that something will occur nor is it a reasonable basis for founding a research project. There is an uncountably infinite class of possibilities which will never be realized. Surely one cannot justify human effort, however pure and devoted to "basic" research, simply on the grounds that the object of the research is a member of such a class.

A wonderful account of what happens when someone takes seriously the notion of pure mathematical possibility as a guide to future actions or occurrences was written some years ago by Russell Maloney.[4] The account begins by describing a critic who "polishes off" an author by saying, "Of course, he wrote one good novel. It's not surprising. After all, we know that if six chimpanzees were set to work pounding six typewriters at random, they would, in a million years, write all the books in the British Museum."[5] One of his listeners, a simple man with a great respect for science, checks the statement with a mathematician who assures him that it is "a perfectly sound popularization of a principle known to every schoolboy who had studied the science of probabilities."[6] With this assurance the man decides to aid the progress of science. He procures six chimpanzees and six typewriters, puts them in a room and waits for results. Then, strictly in accordance with mathematical possibility, the chimpanzees first type out *"Oliver Twist,* and continue with *The Prose of John Donne,* some Anatole France, Conan Doyle, Galen, the collected plays of Somerset Maugham, Marcel Proust, the memoirs of the late Marie of Rumania, and a monograph by a Dr. Wiley on the marsh grasses of Maine and Massachusetts."[7] The mathematician who is called in is somewhat shaken. The fact that the chimpanzees typed sense instead of gibberish, he noted, could be an accident like tossing a hundred consecutive "heads" on a coin, which is perfectly in accord with the statement that the probability of a head is one-half. Nevertheless, as the experiment continues, the chimpanzees never do type gibberish and seem fairly embarked on typing all the books in the British Museum. The mathematician loses his mind, shoots the experimenter and the chimpanzees, and is shot by the experimenter. As the curtain falls on this "Goetterdaemmerung," the last chimpanzee, bleeding to death, ". . . slumped

18   Possibility as a Guide

before his typewriter. Painfully, he looked from the machine to the completed last page of Florio's *Montaigne*. Groping for a fresh sheet, he inserted it, and typed with one finger, 'Uncle Tom's Cabin, by Harriet Beecher Stowe, Chapte. . . .' Then he too was dead." [8]

It might be considered inappropriate to devote so much space to a *New Yorker* spoof, but as Oscar Wilde has noted, nature imitates art. No novelist ever imagined anything so fantastic but that he wasn't outdone by a reputable scientist. It is quite common now to give Jules Verne credit for most of our recent scientific advances. And the chimpanzee argument has recently been used by W. Ross Ashby in Princeton University's *Annals of Mathematics Studies* to prove that machines have intelligence which can be amplified by increasing the finite probability of a meaningful output from a random input:

It has often been remarked that any random sequence, if long enough, will contain *all* the answers. Nothing prevents a child from doodling
$$\cos^2 x + \sin^2 x = 1,$$
or a dancing mote in the sunlight from emitting the same message in Morse or a similar code. Let us be more definite. If each of the above thirteen symbols might have been any one of fifty letters and elementary signs, then as 50^{13} is approximately 2^{73}, the equation can be given in coded form by 73 binary symbols. Now consider a cubic centimeter of air as a turmoil of colliding molecules. A particular molecule's turnings after collision, sometimes to the left and sometimes to the right, will provide a series of binary symbols, each 73 of which, on some given code, either will or will not represent the equation. A simple calculation from the known facts shows that the molecules in every cubic centimeter of air are emitting this sequence *correctly* over a hundred thousand times a second. The objection that "such things don't happen" cannot stand.

Doodling, then, or any other random activity, is capable of producing all that is required.⁹

If chimpanzees can type all the books in the British Museum in a finite time, undoubtedly they can also translate them and write *Uncle Tom's Cabin* in Arabic, and all Russian scientific books in English. And this conjecture, too, is considered by some to be more than fanciful; it is advanced quite seriously by Warren Weaver in his Memorandum which inaugurated most of the present activity in machine translation:

> A more general basis for hoping that a computer could be designed which would cope with a useful part of the problem of translation is to be found in a theorem which was proved in 1943 by McCulloch and Pitts. This theorem states that a robot (or a computer) constructed with regenerative loops of a certain formal character is capable of deducing any legitimate conclusion from a finite set of premises . . . insofar as written language is an expression of logical character, this theorem assures one that the problem is at least formally solvable.¹⁰

Let it be assumed that the McCulloch-Pitts theorem, like the writing ability of the chimpanzees, is logically correct. John Von Neumann has pointed out that such a deduction might involve "thousands or millions or altogether impractical numbers of volumes" and might be much more complicated than the connections of the brain which McCulloch and Pitts were attempting to explain. Von Neumann concludes that tracing all the connections of the physical brain might be a relatively simple way of explaining a formal McCulloch-Pitts net and that such a net is useless as an explanation of human action. In precise logical terms, Von Neumann concludes that the McCulloch-Pitts results are not "effective."

20   Possibility as a Guide

But this matter should be carried further, since it has a direct bearing on the answer to question (1), which is the subject of the following chapter.

According to Weaver, a computer of a certain formal kind is capable of deducing any legitimate conclusion from a finite set of premises. If "legitimate" means legitimate in terms of the premises this statement is certainly true. But if by legitimate is meant "any true statement" then it follows from Goedel's results that given any computer with any finite set of premises, there will be legitimate statements which are not deducible from them. In other words, in terms of Goedel's result, given a McCulloch-Pitts net with any finite set of premises, and a finite number of rules of inference, then there will be an infinite class of true statements which are not deducible from such a net. As a matter of fact, a re-examination of the McCulloch and Pitts paper discloses that not only is the physiological model on which it is based hopelessly inadequate, but that the logical structure is incomplete, full of undefined terms, and even downright mistakes.

The McCulloch-Pitts paper [11] was an important paper because it suggested fruitful analogies between truth-functional logic and models of neurological behavior. But when it is used as a basis for the view that human action, including human thought and natural language, can be completely formalized, *i.e.*, representable as a set of theorems deduced from the McCulloch-Pitts axioms, it becomes scientifically suspect. When it is further offered by McCulloch as a solution of the problem of induction [12] and by Weaver as providing formal assurance that natural languages can be mechanized, it becomes a scientific aberration. How widespread and pervasive such an aberration can become is illustrated in the following two chapters.

3 MECHANICAL TRANSLATION

There is at present a great deal of work going on in the field of mechanical translation. This work would certainly not be justified unless the answer to question (1) was "yes." The fact that research is going on does not in itself mean that the answer is "yes," because there is research going on in the field of extrasensory perception and many very reputable scientists would answer (5) with a flat and unequivocal "no." Further, it is possible, just as in the case of (4) and (5), to so interpret the substantive words in (1) as to make the answer either an unequivocal "no" or an unequivocal "yes." If translation is defined as a nonmechanical activity of the human mind, the answer to (1) is certainly "no," since (1) would reduce to (8). On the other hand, if translation is interpreted as the recognition of code patterns on some sort of physical medium and the manipulation of this medium in terms of different code patterns, *i.e.*, as equivalent to or an extension of the way in which a machine sorts cards, then the answer to (1) would be an unequivocal "yes." There are additional difficulties with the substantive terms of (1). Someone who believed in the nineteenth-century doctrine that man is a machine, could answer (1) with an unequivocal "yes." If man is a machine and man translates from one language to another, then it is certainly possible to translate by machine from one language to another. Both McCulloch and

Oettinger use this nineteenth-century doctrine to insure a positive answer to (1). Thus, the former states: "Since nature has given us a working model, we need not ask whether machines can be built to do what brains can do with information." [1] And the latter adds: "Thus, if our goal is the design of more reliable, more adaptable machines capable of uninterrupted operation over periods of many decades, then living organisms provide, so to speak, an existence theorem guaranteeing the reality of this goal." [2]

Hence, it is seen that the ambiguity of the question resides not only in the word "translation" but in the word "machine." But this is not all, for the notion of language is itself enormously ambiguous. During the nineteenth century and the first half of the present century, when most scientific disciplines sought to be more and more empirical and scientific, the science of linguistics separated itself from classical philology and developed as a science of speech. Its basic concepts of phonemes and morphemes refer to speech and structures of speech; and many scientific linguists hold that written language is an imperfect representation of real and proper linguistic facts, namely, facts of speech. A written symbol, for these scientific linguists, is linguistically significant only as a symbol of sound or sounds. Furthermore, many linguists restricted their interests to a study of sounds and patterns of sounds as purely physical phenomena without involving themselves in normative and nonphysical problems of grammar and meaning. Paralleling this historical development and motivated by the same positivistic bent there was a development of mathematics and logics which concerned itself with purely formal "languages," that is, languages which consist solely and completely of marks on paper and rules for their manipulation. Regarding these languages,

Mechanical Translation 23

questions of meaning are essentially irrelevant and can be dismissed into realms of metalanguages. This development is the basis for Bertrand Russell's aphorism that in mathematics we never know what we are talking about, nor whether what we say is true.

The advent of mechanical translation has had a curious result on these parallel historical developments. Mechanical translation is concerned primarily with *equivalences in meaning of written languages.* Hence it would seem to be the province of neither symbolic logic nor scientific linguistics. Nevertheless, some logicians and linguists are now engaged in research in mechanical translation. Reluctantly, one must agree with George Crabbe that "Fashion, though Folly's child, and guide of fools, Rules e'en the wisest and in learning rules."[3]

It should be clear that the ambiguity of the terms "machine," "language," and "translation" is such that by properly choosing meanings it is possible to answer question (1) with an unequivocal "yes" or an unequivocal "no." If meanings were chosen that made the answer "no," it would follow that millions of dollars had been spent and scarce scientific manpower had been diverted by our government and by private foundations in the pursuit of an impossible result. But it is certain that anyone who attempted to advance such an argument in order to limit research activities would be accused of sophistry, and rightly so. On the other hand, the reverse is also true. Anyone who attempted to justify research activities by definition would be guilty of sophistry in just the same sense.

Hence, if anyone is genuinely concerned with the worthwhileness of research in the field of mechanical translation, he must undertake to go beyond definitions and investigate the original justification for inaugurating such research, the degree of success measured against the original claims, and the real, in addition to the logical, prospects for eventual success.

It has often been asserted that many important scientific discoveries have resulted from accidental observations during the course of a research effort devoted to entirely different ends. This assertion, if true, certainly establishes the value of serendipity, and may justify, after the fact, effort spent on a fruitless investigation; but one should not embark on an investigation which, *prima facie,* is doomed to failure solely in the hope that there may be valuable accidental discoveries. Nevertheless, the appeal to serendipity has become very prevalent in the mechanical translation field.

At the recent hearings on mechanical translation by the Special Investigating Sub-Committee, Committee on Science and Astronautics, United States House of Representatives, most of the witnesses testified that "even if their work in automatic language translation should end in failure, they hoped to contribute to an understanding of language and perhaps to the solution of problems in the field of information storage and retrieval." A recent book on mechanical translation presents a similar justification: "Indeed the future value of research on automatic translation might well hinge more on its contributions to a fundamental understanding of all levels of language structure and of the nature of automatic information processing than on any resulting machine reproduced translations." [4] In the investigation of mechanical translation which is here undertaken, an attempt will be made to be as thorough as possible. It is hoped that the thoroughness will not give rise to tedium. It is fortunate that there is available the book, *Machine Translation of Lan-*

Mechanical Translation 25

guages (hereafter referred to as *MTL*), published in 1955,[5] which gives a complete history of mechanical translation up to the date of its publication; and it is possible to trace subsequent work as reported to the National Science Foundation and listed in the section on mechanical translation in *Current Research and Development in Scientific Documentation*. There is also available a very curious *Report on the State of Machine Translation in the United States and Great Britain*, by Yehoshua Bar-Hillel.

There is one final disclaimer, before getting down to detail. Everyone knows the story of the farmer who saw a camel at a fair and exclaimed, "There ain't no such animal." The one thing which would make this whole investigation supererogatory is the *existence* of a genuine product of mechanical translation. Unfortunately, all the results which were envisioned in 1946 when mechanical translation began are still to be realized and must be investigated as predictions rather than performances. Even Oettinger finds it necessary to conclude his discussion of automatic language translation by noting that: "While several rules for producing smooth Russian-English automatic translations have been proposed in the literature, published experimental results have been conspicuously absent—discounting several newspaper reports that have never been adequately substantiated in the technical literature."[6]

In the Historical Introduction to *MTL*, the following is presented as both the meaning and aim of mechanical translation (hereafter referred to as MT):

In much of the work that follows it is tacitly assumed that a one-to-one correspondence exists between the language of the original text and that of the translation. If this assumption is correct, then it is possible to envisage a purely mechanical process—in the broad sense—which if applied to the input text will result in an output translation, and which if re-applied to the translation will reproduce the original input text.[7]

The passage goes on to indicate that such an ideal result may not be "possible in general" but the section concludes by viewing MT as a continuous development from automatic dictionaries to a complete mechanization of input and "an exact and unambiguous output."

The original idea of the possibility of MT arose in 1946 during a conversation between Warren Weaver and A. D. Booth which dealt with possible applications of computers. In the following year Booth and D. H. V. Britten worked out a "detailed code" for dictionary translation. In 1948 R. H. Richens advanced the idea of shortening an automatic dictionary by storing word stems in one portion of the dictionary and word endings in others, on the grounds that storing stems and possible endings separately would result in a smaller dictionary than one which stored all forms of inflected words. In other words: stems + endings < stems × endings. Richens was apparently unaware that the time required to find a word in a store comprised of "stems + endings" might be much longer than the time required to find a word in a store comprised of "stems × endings." However, Booth and Locke point out that as storage possibilities increased, the desirability of separate stores for stems and endings would decrease.

In 1949 Warren Weaver's memorandum, "Translation," appeared and resulted in the inauguration of research activities at the University of Washington, the University of California, and Massachusetts Institute of Technology. According to Booth, there were a few scoffers but the general reaction to Weaver's memorandum was enthusiastic.

The next major advance was the concept of a pre-editor

and a post-editor, put forward by Erwin Reifler in 1950. The pre-editor prepares the text for the machine; the post-editor prepares the machine output for human consumption. Once it was realized that the cost of pre-editing might be more than the cost of translation itself the pre-editor part of this major advance was abandoned by most workers in the field, including Reifler. In 1951 V. A. Oswald, Jr. and Stewart L. Fletcher published a specific "Proposal for Mechanical Resolution of German Syntax Patterns" using the Standards Western Automatic Computer (SWAC) of the National Bureau of Standards. In the same year Yehoshua Bar-Hillel became the first full-time research worker in the field, being appointed to such a position at Massachusetts Institute of Technology.

The historical account can be departed from at this point to note that in 1959 Bar-Hillel reported to the National Science Foundation

> . . . that no purely automatic procedure is available or in view that would enable presently existing (nonlearning) computers to resolve the polysemy of the word "pen" in such sentences as "The pen is in the box," and "The box is in the pen," within the same contexts that would enable a human reader (or translator) to resolve it immediately and unerringly.[8]

This statement doesn't say that MT is impossible; nor does it even say that purely automatic MT will not be practical tomorrow. The phrase "available or in view" merely condemns as useless all the work of Bar-Hillel's colleagues, many of whom entered the MT field because of his example.

In 1952 a grant from the Rockefeller Foundation made it possible to hold a four-day conference at the Massachusetts Institute of Technology of all those who were known to be active in research in MT. Athough the conference issued no formal conclusions, it was generally agreed that it should be possible to proceed towards translation by a machine in two steps: (1) The construction of an automatic dictionary at the end of approximately twelve months; and (2) the immediate operational analysis of syntax with the view of preparing programs for machine operation. Although it is possible and indeed feasible to construct automatic dictionaries, it is noteworthy that no *working* dictionary has been constructed in the eight years since the conference. Programs have been written for selected vocabularies and selected operations, but no programs exist which would make it possible to translate any arbitrarily selected text from one language to another.

Work on MT continued in 1953; and 1954 was marked by two major events: a demonstration of the IBM-701 ability to translate from Russian into English using a total vocabulary of 250 words and six rules of syntax; and the appearance of Volume I, Number 1, of the journal, *MT* (*Mechanical Translation*).

The book *MTL* appeared in 1955. This book contains most of the major articles written through 1955 plus an annotated bibliography of the first three numbers of *Mechanical Translation*. The major papers from *Mechanical Translation* are reprinted in the book.

The first chapter of the book is a reprint of Warren Weaver's memorandum, "Translation" which, as noted above, can be regarded as the document which inaugurated research in this field. This memorandum makes three basic points: It refers to the McCulloch-Pitts proof as establishing the logical possibility of mechanical translation. The validity of this argument has already been examined.

Secondly, the memorandum discusses the relationship of

meaning to *context* and indicates that this relationship could be studied by investigating "the statistical semantic character of language." Here "statistical" refers not to frequency of usage but to the relative length of phrases required to reduce ambiguity of meaning. Assuming that context has a considerable bearing on ambiguity of meaning, there is a further question concerning the minimum context that has any meaning at all. Bertrand Russell, Willard Van Orman Quine, and most modern analytical philosophers have argued that the *sentence*, rather than the *word*, is the minimum carrier of meaning. This would mean that in mechanical translation, the elements stored would have to be sentences, rather than words. V. H. Yngve has pointed out that there are probably 10^{50} English sentences of twenty words or less. Hence, if the sentence is the basic carrier of meaning, we are about 45 orders of magnitude away from effective mechanical translation. It is certainly the case that parts of sentences, phrases, or words, seem to have meaning in the ordinary understanding of "meaning." On the other hand, there are many contexts in which the meaning of a sentence is derived from the meaning of a paragraph. For every case in which we could store less than a sentence as the carrier of meaning, it would probably be necessary to have a similar number of cases in which it would be necessary to store multiple sentences or paragraphs as units of meaning. Those workers in the field of MT who have presumed that meaning could be handled merely by storing words and endings plus syntactical rules have overlooked an essential element in the semantic discussions in modern logic.

The third point made by Dr. Weaver is that since computers were effective in cryptographic work during the war, there is a presumption that they can be effective in mechanical translation. This presumption is based upon the notion that cryptography is a kind of translation. The error in this analogy resides in the fact that in cryptography there are no dictionaries or any initial indication of the language represented by the code. Hence, one of the first steps in cryptography is the rearrangement of the code in as many different orders as possible in order to look for patterns and repetition of code elements. If a cryptographer had available to him a knowledge of the language represented by an intercepted message and a dictionary of that language, not to speak of multilingual dictionaries between that language and any other, it would never occur to him to use a computer to write his translation. In the field of mechanical translation, it is assumed that computers will be used to translate between known languages concerning which bilingual dictionaries exist. Hence, the analogy between cryptography and mechanical translation is certainly false in its essentials. On all three points the Weaver memorandum fails to provide a rational or a feasible report for the enterprise of mechanical translation.

The balance of the papers in *MTL* consists of various discussions of language, syntax, grammar, semantic units, meaning, etc., together with some descriptions of experiments. The experiments were not definitive and they could only be considered important if they followed from a valid theory of language, meaning, and translation. What such a valid theory might be is nowhere evidenced in this volume. Some examples will illustrate this fact. Richens and Booth begin their discussion of the general principles of mechanical translation by noting that, "A language is a series of symbols representing ideas." [9] Such a definition could only be advanced by someone ignorant or disdainful of all that has been

Mechanical Translation   31

said on this subject in the last 2500 years. In any case, the accepted modern view is that the symbol "Washington Monument" refers to a physical structure on the Mall in Washington and not to anybody's idea of that physical structure. Richens and Booth continue with the following: "The simplest conceivable written language would have one symbol per idea." [10]

This last statement should be considered in connection with the article by Dodd on "Model English." [11] Dodd proposes to describe some rules for a model language for the purposes of mechanical translation. In this model language every word would have just one meaning and every meaning would be expressible in just one word; that is, there would be a one-to-one correspondence between a set of meanings and a set of words. It is a simple matter to demonstrate that Dodd's "Model English" as an extension of the Richens-Booth concept of one symbol per idea results in a language in which there would be no synonymy, no dictionaries, and no reference to the physical world. A dictionary defines a word in terms of a synonym, in terms of a set of words and a context, or by using an illustration. If each word had only one meaning and each meaning were expressible in just one word, it would be impossible to state in words what any word meant.

The views expressed by Richens, Booth, and Dodd concerning the relations of symbols to ideas and meanings are distinguished from other views in this book not in being jejune, but only in being more explicitly jejune. One more example may be considered. Reifler, in discussing the mechanical determination of meaning, states that the MT linguist ". . . need not adhere strictly to the results of scientific language research. When they serve his purpose, he will consider them. But he will ignore them when an arbitrary treatment of the language material better serves his purpose." [12] This is certainly a *reductio ad absurdum* of the enterprise of mechanical translation. It is to be an enterprise which starts not from a scientific study of language, but from an arbitrary determination of what a language is in the terms required to make mechanical translation a scientifically valid enterprise. Reifler's statement bears out the early observation that MT requires a new fashion in logic and linguistics designed to make its extravagances respectable.

The work in MT since 1955 is reported by the National Science Foundation and evaluated by Bar-Hillel. Taken as a body it consists of a set of attempts to resolve ambiguities in meaning by formal syntactical analysis of various natural languages: English, Russian, German, Chinese, etc. The formal analysis is required to make possible the writing of programs for a computer which would effectively translate from an input in one language to an output in another. There has also been some work on an interlingua, *i.e.*, a common machine language which would mediate between all natural languages in the mechanical translation process.

There are two ways in which this work can be evaluated. The problem of mechanical translation can be treated as a formal problem and there can be a logical query concerning the possibility of a solution to such a problem. On the other hand, mechanical translation can be treated as a practical problem and in practical terms this problem can be succinctly stated as follows: Is it cheaper to use mechanical dictionaries and programmed computers to achieve a passable imitation of human translation than it is to breed and train human translators or even to breed whole generations of multilingual people?

Mechanical Translation 33

Much of what has been said in the previous chapter about the formal possibilities of questions (9) and (10), about Goedel's proof, and Von Neumann's discussions of the effectiveness of the McCulloch-Pitts conclusions applies here to the question of the theoretical possibility of mechanical translation. This application has already been noted with reference to the statement by Weaver that the problem of mechanical translation is formally solvable.

Even without reference to such difficult and erudite matters there is a simple consideration that will establish that mechanical translation is formally impossible. A formal system must utilize the principles of substitutivity and equivalence. That is, if Language A is to be formally (mechanically) translatable into Language B, there must be at some level a one-to-one relation of synonymy between elements of A and elements of B. This requirement was duly envisioned in the passage by Booth commented on above. The one-to-one relation of synonymy might be asserted to exist between the words of A and B, the phrases of A and B, the sentences of A and B, the syntactic structures of A and B, the paragraphs of A and B, etc. The question is: Is any one of these assertions true? No one in MT seriously supposes that such one-to-one relationships exist between any pairs of natural languages or even between a natural language and a formal language such as arithmetic or the language of the propositional calculus.

In the absence of a one-to-one relation of synonymy between the definable elements of one language and the definable elements of another, human translation is still possible. It is generally recognized that two translations of a passage into any language by different people might both be adequate translations of the passage and yet both might differ from each other in terms of the words used, the phrases used, the sentences used, and, in general, the total syntax of the paragraphs. It might be thought that the fact that human beings translate in just this manner, that is, a manner involving nonequivalence of one language to another, is *prima facie* evidence for the fact that it is formally possible for machines to translate without requiring equivalence between elements of languages. The difficulty here resides in the notion of formal. It is necessary at this point to expand the discussion in Chapter 1, and to refer to the historical opposition between *intuitionists* and *formalists* in the field of mathematics.

At the present time it seems that by virtue of Goedel's proof and similar developments in logic and mathematics, the intuitionists have the upper hand and the formalists are on the defensive, even though most of the activity in modern logic consists of attempts to elaborate various limited formal systems permitted by Goedel's proof and the development which led up to it. The work of Z. S. Harris and Noam Chomsky, which will be discussed in the next chapter, represents an attempt to regard natural language as a formal system, even though Alfred Tarski, a formalist, says that this is impossible. Since, at the very least, language must include all mathematics and since there seems to be a proof that all mathematics is not susceptible to formal treatment, it would follow that natural language is not susceptible to formal treatment. This situation affects the problem of mechanical translation and human translation as follows: We assume that machines are not capable of intuition. Hence, if they are to translate at all, they must translate formally. On the other hand, not even the most rigorous formalist in mathematics ever seriously denied that human beings have intuitions, even if he hoped to show that mathematical development could proceed independently of such intuitions. *Intuitions,* in this context, are meant to be nothing more mysterious than experiences and feelings. To say that a human being translates nonformally is to say that in any act of translation he will make use of nonformal deliverances of his experience and feeling. There are some who might argue against this conclusion by asserting that the verbalization of experiences and feelings involves their formalization. This is the McCulloch-Pitts argument to the effect that whatever is expressible, as opposed to experienceable, can be modeled in a McCulloch-Pitts nerve net. The final answer on this point is that there is not the slightest evidence for the equivalence of experience and verbal expression. Their equivalence could only be asserted by someone who had denied his own humanity, by someone who had never listened to music, looked at a painting, fallen in love, or been absorbed in a natural scene. With so much it can be concluded that mechanical translation in the formal sense is impossible because translation in the formal sense from one natural language to another is impossible. We are brought, then, to this problem: is mechanical translation possible as a practical approach for providing relatively adequate expressions of the meaning of one language in another?

Let it be supposed that corresponding to the human ability to translate intuitively is the machine capability to translate by approximation. *Approximation* is meant to be the strict mathematical process of approaching a limit which in principle can never be reached. For example, if context is a determinant of meaning, a mechanical dictionary can be designed which stores as units not single words but two-word combinations, three-word combinations, phrases, whole sentences, etc. If, as most modern logicians would assert, the basic carrier of meaning is the sentence, and our present computer stores are about forty-five orders of magnitude away from the required size for a sentence dictionary, and if the general capability of computers increases by an order of magnitude every ten years, the requisite size computer stores may be available in 450 years.

If it is said that some words and phrases have meaning independently of their inclusion in a particular sentence, it must also be said that for some purposes contexts larger than sentences would have to be stored as units. Obviously, there is neither profit nor practical result to be expected from a brute force attack on the translation problem by increasing the size of contexts in the store.

Another "practical" approach to mechanical translation is the attempt to develop computer programs which will determine the syntax of a sentence by examining, not the context, but such characteristics of a sentence as word order, word endings, phrase structure, etc. There is a possibility worth noting here that this whole approach is viciously circular, since it is more reasonable to suppose that parts of speech, word order, endings—or, in general, the syntactical character of the parts of a sentence—are determined by the meaning of the sentence rather than that the meaning of a sentence is determined by the syntactical properties of its parts. In ordinary grammatical studies a sentence is analyzed to show *how* the meaning has been expressed, not to determine *what* the meaning is. Unless there is prior understanding of the meaning of the sentence, grammatical analysis cannot take place. For example, we proceed from an understanding of the meaning of a word to the recognition that it is the subject of a sentence. We could not know which "sign" was the subject

Mechanical Translation 37

of a sentence if we did not know the meaning of the signs.

On the direct and uncomplicated question of the practicality, as contrasted with the theoretical justification, of computer programs for the analysis of syntax and the determination of meaning, the obvious approach is to search for the existence of any such programs. The search has been made and it can be stated categorically that twelve years after the Warren Weaver memorandum no practical, usable MT computer program exists. As noted above, there does not even exist a practical or usable mechanical dictionary. And this is not for lack of effort. Bar-Hillel has calculated that the annual expenditure for research in MT, exclusive of machine costs, is approximately $3,000,000 per year. Measured against the billion dollar federal budgets it may seem a small amount, but it is sufficient to run a medium-sized university. It is sufficient to hire 300 full-time translators at $10,000 per year, or to train 300 translators at a $10,000 training cost per translator. Over the years this would produce a reasonably sized body of competent translators, especially if it is added to the present annual expenditure for training in languages. Furthermore, training in languages may remove the need for translation.

It is wrong to assume that if machines could translate they could do so without cost. Computers are very expensive and the writing and "de-bugging" (testing and re-writing) of programs is more so. In addition, the preparation of a machine-readable code from a printed text is a costly operation. It has been said by the most committed believers in mechanical translation that mechanical translation will never be economically feasible unless a "print reader" is developed that will convert printed text automatically to punched cards or to some other form of machine-readable code. There are *readers* which can cope with standard fonts in standard positions and sizes; but no one has yet designed or made a *reader* which can handle any font that comes along. The Post Office can reasonably ask its clients to standardize the position and type of marks on envelopes in return for special handling privileges; but it seems more reasonable to ask the Russians to supply us with English abstracts of their publications than to ask that they standardize their fonts and typography to make things easier for our designers of print readers.

If it is the case, headlines in the popular press or even articles in reputable scientific journals notwithstanding, that mechanical translation *is* not successful, are there any good reasons to suppose that at some future time it *will be?* In short, what is the evidence that an economically feasible mechanical translation can be achieved in the immediate or near future?

Bar-Hillel's conclusions and recommendations on this point should be revealing, since they are based on a government-sponsored study of all of the major MT projects; and he is, after all, one of the early enthusiasts who started this whole business. He says: "For the time being, research on MT proper should only concern itself with supplying mechanical aids to translation, while aiming at constantly improving these aids and increasing their number." [13]

Mechanical aids are of many kinds, namely, fountain pens as opposed to quill pens; electric typewriters as opposed to manual typewriters; dictionary stands as opposed to human laps; rotary filing cabinets as opposed to cardboard boxes; and even electric lights as opposed to oil lamps or candles. Concerning such mechanical aids, there exists fairly good evidence that they will contribute to the efficiency of human translators.

It must not be supposed that this exegesis is fanciful and that Bar-Hillel obviously intended to imply that computers would or should constitute the mechanical aids to human translators. There is little evidence that computers can do any such thing, and Bar-Hillel himself doesn't recommend them. He continues: "The economic basis of a commercial partly-mechanized translation center would be strengthened by the development of a reliable print reader and the construction of a special-purpose translation machine."[14] Bar-Hillel does not suggest the use of any existing computers, but "the construction of a special-purpose translation machine." It may be permitted at this point to ask: "What *is* a special-purpose translation machine?" Has anyone ever designed or built one? Does Bar-Hillel know how to design or build one? If one could be designed and built, would it, by definition, produce adequate translations? One may call a card sorter a data processing machine, but one does not thereby change its capacity to sort cards. A train can be called "Der Fliegende Frankfurter" but it remains a train and doesn't thereby become an airborne sausage. It is supererogatory to note further with reference to this passage that reliable print readers exist which are of no aid to translation; and that there is no existing economic basis for a commercial partly mechanized translation center. One might create what did not exist, but it is difficult to see how a nonexisting commercial operation could be strengthened.

As has been noted before and will be noted again and again in this volume as we run to earth certain fashionable scientific aberrations, it is necessary to analyze the aberration to the point of tedium. Otherwise, it gets enshrined in the literature, is quoted and referenced, and before a computer can print "Jack Robinson," a "scientific" literature exists.

From Bar-Hillel's *Report on the State of Machine Translation in the United States and Great Britain*, it is impossible to discover the evidences for the practicality of mechanical translation, although it is clear that he thinks that research in this field should be directed towards practical, as opposed to theoretical, goals. He admits that the aim he recommends makes the field uninteresting and expects that neither he nor anyone else interested in "basic" problems will have any interest in achieving it. Bar-Hillel knows that the degree of achievement of a practical goal, *e.g.*, the actual production of economically feasible, semantically adequate mechanical translation, is measurable by many who cannot follow him into the arcane areas of logic; and it is clear he does not wish to subject his own work to such measurement.

In his 1955 volume on MT, Booth gave some cost figures on a method of word-for-word translating using punched card equipment. The cost was twice the cost of human translation. Since that time few of the researchers in the field have thought it worthwhile to undertake similar studies of the practical problem of mechanical translation.

Recently one of the oldest and largest centers of activity in MT issued its magnum opus covering two years of research from May, 1956 to June, 1958.[15] One of the sections of this work is a study of "The design of a practical Russian-English mechanical translator," [16] and another discusses "Some of the economics of machine translation." [17] The former is typical of many papers in this field in that it does not present a design, but merely discusses some of the problems involved in achieving a design. Its practicality consists in some estimates of desirable rates of dictionary look-up. But it gives no cost

Mechanical Translation   41

comparisons for human and mechanical translation; hence, its notion of practicality is vacuous. The latter paper does make an attempt to estimate the comparative cost of per word translation of human and mechanical translation. It indicates that there are four major areas of cost in mechanical translation: (1) Preparation of the text material for the machine; (2) Dictionary search and the production of the first crude word-for-word translation; (3) Logical processing to improve the first word-for-word translation; and (4) Printout of the improved word-for-word translation. A rough estimate of these costs indicates that without an electronic print reader, mechanical translation will be twice as expensive as human translation and therefore "*cannot* be justified on the basis of cost alone." It seems that the main area of research should be print readers and not translating machines. This, of course, shifts the problem from: "Is mechanical translation a practical objective?" to: "Are print readers capable of reading any size and font of type a practical objective?" Maybe they are, although here again there is no real evidence for an affirmative answer. In any case, the impracticality of mechanical translation is conceded; and research in the field of mechanical translation, as contrasted with research in the field of print readers, has little prospect of modifying the situation. In the last analysis, the print reader gambit is a red herring. It distracts those responsible for research in MT from facing the central fact that nowhere in the literature of MT is there a systems engineering study of its feasibility or practicality. In the absence of such a study and in light of the known informality of language and meaning, research in MT takes on the character not of genuine scientific investigation, but of a romantic quest such as the search for the Holy Grail.

4   LEARNING-MACHINES

About a year ago the author was privileged to sit one evening with a group of data processing experts who were attending an institute in Poughkeepsie. Conversation turned to learning-machines. Most of those present had no doubts that machines capable of learning would soon be built. When questions were posed concerning the nature of learning in men and machines and whether or not learning in one was similar or identical to learning in the other, a curious fact emerged. There was considerable agreement among those present concerning the nature of learning in machines, but wide disagreement concerning the nature of human learning. There was agreement that the term "learning," when applied to human behavior, was vague and ill-defined in spite of the efforts of psychologists to evolve theories of learning. Out of all this a curious consensus emerged. Just because "learning" had no definite meaning when used to describe human behavior and did have a definite meaning when used to describe the activity of a machine, it seemed reasonable to accept the definition which applied to machines and to extend the same definition to cover human action. In other words, man-machine identity is achieved not by attributing human attributes to the machine, but by attributing mechanical limitations to man. From one point of view, it doesn't matter very much whether the leveling is down or up, so long as the end of the process is the assertion of man-machine identity. But if this identity seems on one hand abhorrent and on the other, literally and completely unscientific, an understanding of the process by which such a doctrine is developed and given an air of cogency will help in reversing the process and exhibiting its character as a scientific aberration.

When learning is used with reference to machines, it has the specific meaning of "improvement of performance based upon past performance." There are many machines for which a program can be written to change part of its own instructions on the basis of feeding its output back into the machine. There are some theorists who go beyond this and assert that even without a detailed program, a machine can be constructed which will modify its behavior to improve its probability of producing certain outputs, if the desirability of these outputs is one of the facts given to the machine in its initial state.

Machine-learning, if it occurs, would of necessity be a formal process in the sense of *formal* mathematics. This, as has been noted, is also true of mechanical translation; and in this case, as in the discussion of mechanical translation, it is necessary to ask whether there is any reason to assume that human learning is merely a formal process. Even if human learning is in part formal, it also may be much more, in which case the word "learning" would not have the same meaning when applied to men and machines. The identity "human learning $=$ machine learning" would be false in just the same sense that the identity "all numbers $=$ whole numbers" is false. It is easy to see that the latter identity is false because it is easy to give examples of numbers that are not whole numbers. In the same sense, it is necessary to give

44   Learning-Machines

examples of human learning that are not formal or mechanical.

This task can begin by first noting that the doctrine of conditioned reflexes as an explanation of human habits and human learning is another instance of a widespread scientific aberration. Sir Charles Sherrington can be accepted as an authority that although the behavior of living organisms can be modified by subjecting them to certain patterns of experience, reflexes in the physiological sense of that term are not conditionable or modifiable. In short, the expression "conditioned reflex" is a contradiction, because physiologists distinguish reflex activity from other types of nervous activity on the basis of the fact that reflexes cannot be conditioned. There is nothing stranger or more mysterious in this fact than there is in the denial of the Lamarckian doctrine of the inheritance of acquired characteristics. Sherrington explicitly and categorically distinguishes reflex behavior from habitual behavior on the grounds that habitual behavior is acquired and modifiable, whereas reflex behavior is not. If Pavlov wanted to condition a reflex he should have worked on something simple like the knee jerk, instead of the salivation of dogs. Pavlov, in his famous experiments, did not modify the salivation reflex. He merely modified its conscious stimulation. If a dog salivates when he expects to eat, he will salivate if the sound of a bell makes him expect to eat. The experiment seems to prove that the reflex is unmodifiable even when the conscious stimulation is drastically modified.

Even though this reference to Sherrington's and Pavlov's work seems to be quite beyond the basic theme of this chapter, it is made to illustrate a point. Turing says in one place that he will not pay much attention to the mathematical argument against the ability of machines to think (or learn) because those who are prone to deny these abilities to machines are not the kind of people who use—or are impressed by—mathematical arguments. Turing preferred to concentrate his fire against those who object to his conclusions on religious or moral grounds. Thus Turing lent his support to the gratuitous and false assumption advanced by many other computer enthusiasts that all the scientific literature is what William James called "tough-minded" and is on the side of those who belittle life and glorify mechanics.

Mathematical considerations and physiological considerations are of basic importance in any discussion of machine learning. And most of the bad mathematics and bad physiology which have been accumulated around this question have been contributed by those who assert the identity of machine learning and human learning. For example: In "Automata Studies" in the *Annals of Mathematics Studies,* the editors published two papers by Albert M. Uttley on "Conditional Probability Machines and Conditioned Reflexes." These papers are introduced by the following general statement:

An important characteristic of animal behaviour is that the same motor response can be evoked by a variety of different configurations of the world external to the animal. For the animal these configurations resemble one another in some respect. Similarly there can be variation in the motor response, and different responses resemble one another. In this paper, it is suggested that this "resemblance" consists of two known mathematical relations: the first is the *inclusive* relation of Set *Theory;* the second relation is that of *conditional probability*. From these two relations are deduced the principles of design of a machine, whose reactions to stimuli are similar in a number of ways to those of an animal; . . .[1]

Considering first the *inclusive* relation of set theory, Uttley adds: ". . . and in Set Theory no relation is considered between elements of a set other than that of inclusion in it." [2] As a matter of fact, in set theory the relation between a set and its members is not "inclusion" but "membership," which is a very different thing; the relation of "inclusion" holds not between a set and its members, but between sets. Uttley's statement that he deduces the principles of design of a machine from this statement of set theory is true only in the sense that a false proposition implies any proposition. He could have deduced that "The moon is made of green cheese" from such a description of set theory. Further, Uttley's confusion between sets and members infests his whole subsequent discussion of conditional probability and conditioned reflex so that it is literally impossible to understand what he is talking about. Apparently, if one is "politically right" on the question of conditioned reflexes and machine learning, it is not necessary to be right mathematically, even in the *Annals of Mathematics Studies*.

Corresponding to Uttley's vague mathematics, some equally vague physiology of conditioned reflexes and learning-machines was introduced quite early into the literature by Wiener:

> I wish to emphasize that I do not say that the process of the conditioned reflex operates according to the mechanism I have given; I merely say that it *could* so operate. If, however, we assume this or any similar mechanism, there are a good many things we can say concerning it. One is that this mechanism is capable of learning. It has already been recognized that the conditioned reflex is a learning mechanism. . . . There is nothing in the nature of the computing machine which forbids it to show conditioned reflexes.[3]

When reputable scientists begin to *accept* explanations merely on the basis that they *could* be true and that nothing *forbids* their being true, science becomes indistinguishable from superstition.

It is not necessary for the purposes of this chapter that the possibility of conditioning reflexes be denied, but only that some behavior be exhibited which is not explainable as a conditioned reflex. And here again it is possible to refer to Sherrington for the physiological distinction between habit and reflex; and to any conscious learning experience as evidence that learning cannot be completely explained as a species of conditioned reflex. Anyone who has ever learned to play the piano knows that his learning consisted of the replacement of *conscious direction* of his fingers by *habitual* (unconscious) *movement* of his fingers. One acceptable definition of learning is the change from conscious to unconscious (habitual) activity to attain a desired goal. Here is a physiological and psychological definition of learning which is as simple and straightforward as "improved performance based on consequences of past performance." If this suggested definition is adopted, then machine learning would imply the existence of a conscious machine which had the ability to develop habits which would change some of its reactions from conscious to unconscious. I see no more reason to adopt such a definition of learning with respect to a machine than I do for accepting the other as a description of human learning. At this point, then, honesty requires that the word "learning" not be used without some qualifying explanation to distinguish human from machine learning.

It is a fact of considerable importance that the literature on machine learning is almost exclusively concerned with learning to play games like Turing's game, checkers, or chess. This is certainly curious. If machines can learn, why restrict their efforts to learning games which are not likely to have significant social implications? Even human chess and checker players are less important socially than football players. Why should multimillion dollar machines be used in pastimes which the machines certainly do not enjoy (or do they)?

The justification for teaching machines to play chess or checkers is usually presented in the following terms. Chess, it is said, is an excellent example of a human activity which is definitely intellectual; and yet which is sufficiently separable or definable to permit limited experiments which will not involve unspecifiable background conditions. This, at first glance, seems an eminently reasonable justification. It is with certain ambiguities in the notion of learning to play a game that the balance of this chapter is concerned.

Let us consider first the game of football. It will readily be admitted that knowing the rules of football is not equivalent to an ability to play football. In other words, concerning football at least, the statements, "John knows the rules of football" and "John can play football" are not equivalent. It may be said here that the reason for this nonequivalence lies in the fact that football is intellectual with respect to the rules, and physical with respect to the ability to play it; but it will be seen that this same distinction holds with reference to games which do not involve physical ability. Consider the game of poker. The rules of poker are very simple. A man could teach his wife the rules of poker in fifteen minutes. On the other hand, knowing the rules of poker and being able to *play* poker are two different things. Bridge, as contrasted with poker, has a much more elaborate system of rules; but here again, it is only after people learn the rules of bridge that they can begin to learn to *play* it. If we go from cards to checkers or chess, the typical computer games, the distinction

Learning-Machines 49

between knowing the rules of a game and knowing how to play the game still stands. Anyone can learn the rules of chess in fifteen minutes, but one cannot learn to *play* chess in fifteen minutes.

It can readily be admitted in this case, as in the case of mechanical translation, that any operation which can be formalized, that is, described by a set of rules, can be handled by a mechanical device. To the extent that a game has formal rules, including not only rules of play, but rules to evaluate the results of play, the game can be played by a machine.

On the other hand, we have it on Claude E. Shannon's authority that the game of chess can be completely formalized. Unfortunately, a computer playing a completely formal game, with the ability to consider 1,000,000 moves per second, would require 10^{95} years to make its first move. In other words, chess is formalized by making every move an instruction according to a rule, and in a forty-move chess game there would be 10^{120} such possible instructions. Since humans can play good chess and can plan long sequences of moves, it seems clear that they do not play formal chess, any more than they play formal poker or translate formally. Hence, it must be insisted that the common-sense distinction between the informal process of learning to play a game and the formal process of learning its rules is valid.

In more general terms, this distinction is, of course, the distinction between learning by precept or rule and learning by experience. The insistence upon "learning by doing" in modern education is an insistence that learning is not a formal process of memorizing and behaving according to rules.

There should be no need, at this point, to reiterate that experience is a conscious process and that human learning based on experience is also a conscious process. But it is still necessary to meet the following type of objection. It will be said that man knows that he learns, but not "how" he learns. "Man can solve problems without knowing how he solves them. This simple fact sets the condition for all attempts to rationalize and understand human decision making and problem solving." [4]

The truism expressed in this and similar statements is that man can do something or other without knowing the exact physiology of what he does. He can move his fingers without knowing how the nerves control the muscles; he can see without understanding how messages are coded and transmitted from the environment to his brain. He can also digest food without knowing how his stomach and intestines operate.

So far as he is interested in "how," any man can study physiology, which is apparently more than the computer experts are prepared to do. But even without studying physiology he can notice a significant difference between seeing or moving his arm, and digesting his food. To see is to be conscious; it is to have a conscious experience whatever the underlying physiology of the process; and a man can move his arm or not as he wills. But he is not conscious of his digestion and he cannot control it by willing. The fact that a man solves problems without, in many cases, understanding the physiology of the solution may be an interesting fact to the metaphysician; it is of no importance to either a man interested in solving any given problem or, for that matter, to the physiologist. The gambit disclosed by such comments is the following: If man doesn't know the underlying physiology of his actions, maybe it is all right to suppose these actions resemble the actions of a computer. Such an argument makes as much sense as supposing that if a man understands

Learning-Machines 51

bicycles and doesn't understand airplanes, he can assert that "airplanes are bicycles."

Turing considers in some detail the "alleged fact" that humans are conscious and machines are not, as constituting a fundamental distinction between the thinking or learning ability of men and machines. He attempts to argue against this distinction on the grounds that anyone who uses this argument must be a solipsist, that is, must assert that only his own consciousness exists. There is no way to answer Turing on this point, any more than one can make a reasonable reply to a string of nonsense syllables. Like Uttley's deduction of machines from a hopelessly confused statement of set theory, Turing's argument for solipsism is incredibly jejune. He may have been a creative mathematician but he was an amateur in philosophy. He illustrates here a common form of scientific aberration, namely, the tendency of computer experts to be pontifical about subjects in which they have no competence. Most of the time the incompetence is in the field of physiology, as in discussions of human learning and conditioned reflexes by mathematicians and electrical engineers. This point cannot be too strongly emphasized.

In three different passages Bar-Hillel notes that what he calls FAHQMT (fully automatic high quality mechanical translation) is not possible unless learning machines ". . . can be built and programs written for them which will endow these machines with quasi-human intelligence, knowledge and knowledgability."[5] Such a statement is no more scientific, and certainly less meaningful, than a statement by a theologian who says we will never attain peace until and unless Christ comes again. It would be more sensible to devote the nation's monetary resources to research looking toward the Second Coming than it would be to support re-

52 *Learning-Machines*

search to solve the problems of FAHQMT by attempting to build learning-machines with intelligence, knowledge, and knowledgeability.

In the final analysis, our electrical engineers and computer enthusiasts should stop talking this way or face the serious charge that they are writing science fiction to titillate the public and to make an easy dollar or a synthetic reputation.

5   THE CLAIMS OF LINGUISTIC ANALYSIS

The separation between philology and descriptive linguistics which has been a hundred years in the making has recently been completely confounded, and one of the worst offenders in this regard is Chomsky. Since he is one of the most highly respected workers in the new area of linguistic analysis or structural linguistics, a detailed study of his work will be rewarding. He begins one of his books by noting quite correctly that for the linguist who is occupied with "studying language as an instrument with almost no concern for the uses to which the instrument is put . . . there is ample justification for rejecting any appeal to meaning in the study of linguistic form." [1] But within the same section he notes that a linguist "avoids semantic foundations in the study of linguistic form for the simple and sufficient reason that this course is apparently the only one that enables him to arrive at a clear insight into grammatical structure." [2] Chomsky to the contrary, grammar in its traditional sense is essentially concerned with meaning and how meaning should be expressed; whereas linguistics deals with the phenomenon of speech as it occurs and has occurred, and has nothing to do with normative grammar. Every schoolboy studies grammar, but very few study linguistics. There are linguists who would insist that linguistics is concerned with syntax and grammar, but they redefine these words so that the phenomena they describe have little to do with traditional syntax and grammar. Chomsky is certainly interested in grammar but, as will be seen, he thinks of grammar not as a set of rules for proper expression, but almost as a physical device involved in actual expression.

Since it is important that in discussing the translation of languages, the notion of a language must be clear, Chomsky's definition of a language repays study. "By a *language* in this discussion is meant a set of sentences all constructed from a finite alphabet of phonemes (or letters)."[3] (For a man who wishes to clarify meanings, Chomsky has an infuriating habit of talking about "phonemes or letters" and "morphemes or words" without indicating whether the "or" is an or of opposition or apposition.) In any case, many students of linguistics would hold that:

(1) A letter (a shape) is not a phoneme (a sound) and a phoneme is not a letter.
(2) There is no such thing as an alphabet of phonemes, although an alphabet as a set of shapes can symbolize a set of sounds.
(3) There is a language of phonemes, and a language made up of sentences made up of words made up of letters, but the *two* languages are not identical, *i.e.*, there is a spoken language and a written language, and they are not identical.
(4) Language, in its basic sense, is made up of sounds and not of sentences.
(5) Sentences, which are ordered sets of words beginning with a capital letter and ending with a period, cannot be constructed out of phonemes, since there are no

capital phonemes nor phonemic periods outside of Victor Borge's monologues.

(6) A finite set of letters can be used in the construction of a set of many languages. Hence *a* language (*e.g.,* English) cannot be defined solely as constructed from such a set.

Next to the notion of language itself, the notions of "grammar," "linguistic structures," and "linguistic transformations" carry the heaviest burden of ambiguity in Chomsky's work, *e.g.,* "The grammar of a language can be viewed as a *theory* [italics mine] of the structure of this language." [4] and "When one speaks of the 'grammar of English' one refers to the device that has been constructed to generate English sentences." [5] One may suppose that apart from the idea of activity implied by the term "generate" it is permissible to equate a "theory" with a "device." On the other hand, to talk of grammar being constructed to generate sentences is as illuminating as the statement that conjugations are constructed to generate verbs.

Progressing beyond these definitions of grammar, Chomsky describes linguistic structures either as "kernel sentences" or as grammatical (*i.e.,* linguistic) transformations of kernel sentences. Chomsky's notion of a "kernel sentence" is such sentences as "John is reading the book" and "They are flying planes." Although there are probably no such entities as kernel sentences, if there were, they would more appropriately be such expressions as Look, What, Ugh, No, Yes, or Maybe. Chomsky's notion of kernel sentences will be discussed below. But even if his notion of proper declarative kernel sentences with noun phrases, verbs, and objects is accepted, the transformations of such sentences are not easy to understand.

56   *Linguistic Analysis*

"John is reading the book," he holds, can be transformed to "Is John reading the book?" And "They are flying planes" can be transformed to "Are they flying planes?" The ambiguity in the meaning of the second sentence and its transformation is an ambiguity which is traceable to an ambiguity in linguistic structure, *i.e.*, They/are/flying planes, or They/are flying/planes.

Contrary to Chomsky's view, this ambiguity is not linguistic but grammatical. If we wish to make a linguistic transformation of "John is reading the book" to a question, we can do so not by transforming the sentence but by modifying our inflection, *e.g.*, John — is reading the book? Certainly changes of tone, like changes of grammar, have a bearing on meaning, as do facial expressions. Every American knows the famous statement of *The Virginian*, "When you say that, smile." The smile or lack of it is a major determinant of meaning in this case, but to regard the smile as a part of grammar or a linguistic transformation in Chomsky's sense is to be simply naïve about a very complicated problem. And dressing up such naïveté with Markov Processes and equations doesn't really help.

Chomsky concludes his analysis by noting that "If the grammar of a language is to provide insight into the way the language is understood, it must be true, in particular, that if a sentence is ambiguous (understood in more than one way) then this sentence is provided with alternative analysis by the grammar." [6]

Grammar certainly provides insight into the way in which a language is understood but not all ambiguity of meaning results from ambiguity of grammar. There is an enormous range of ambiguity derivable from a lack of context, *e.g.*,

Hawaii has many pineapple plants. He took the fifth. He overlooked the solution.

In a recent article Quine has shown that both the definition of a phoneme and the definition of the class of grammatical statements cannot be formally derived without reference to the semantic notions of synonymy and significance. Quine's results, like Goedel's results in another connection, indicate that Chomsky's attempt to develop formal grammar and transformation rules is an attempt to achieve what is strictly and logically impossible. In a certain sense Chomsky himself realized this because he starts his formal description of language by noting: "We shall limit ourselves to English, and shall assume intuitive knowledge of English sentences and nonsentences." [7] In order to see what is implied by such a caveat at the beginning, let us suppose that a treatise on logic began with the observation that it would assume an intuitive knowledge of which combinations of symbols were theorems and which were not theorems. A formal development from this point on is not possible.

Quite apart from the nature of linguistic transformations, Chomsky's position rests on the notion that there are entities which he calls "kernel sentences." A linguistic transformation is an operation on a kernel sentence which changes it to a sentence which is not a kernel sentence; or, contrariwise, it is an operation on a non-kernel sentence which derives the kernel sentence.

It is clear, therefore, that the validity of Chomsky's entire theory of linguistic transformations rests upon the assertion that a class (finite or infinite) of kernel sentences exists and can be described. By "described" is meant that given an instance of a sentence (S), it must be possible by analysis or inspection to decide whether the sentence is a member of the class kernel sentences (*i.e.*, whether S is a member of K). If the determination that S is a member of K is to be made by machine, there is an additional requirement that the truth or falsity of "S is a member of K" be formally, *i.e.*, mechanically, decidable. Chomsky is not very clear concerning the formal decidability of membership in K; but Harris, whose views on kernel sentences will also be examined, is quite specific on the point that a mechanical determination of K sentences is possible and feasible.

Whether membership in K is decidable intuitively, empirically, or formally, there is a common requirement that K have a meaning. For example, if it is said that "linguistic transformations can reduce any given sentence to a shredded wheat sentence," it is necessary not only to know what *shredded wheat* is, for such a statement to be decidable, but also to know what *shredded wheat sentences* are. In short, it doesn't follow that because everyone knows what a kernel is, that anyone knows what a kernel sentence is. Chomsky does not attempt a rigorous definition of kernel sentences. He describes them in passages such as:

When we actually carry out a detailed study of English structure, we find that the grammar can be greatly simplified if we limit the kernel to a very small set of simple declarative sentences (in fact, probably a finite set) such as "The man ate the food," etc.[8]

and

The actual sentences of real life are usually not kernel sentences, but rather complicated transforms of these. We find, however, that the transformations are, by and large, meaning-preserving, so that we can view the kernel sentences underlying a given sentence as being, in some sense, the elementary "content elements" in terms of which the actual transform is "understood." [9]

Linguistic Analysis 59

Transformational analysis, in particular, permits one partially to reduce the problem of explaining how language is understood to that of explaining how kernel sentences are understood, where the kernel sentences underlying a given sentence are thought of as elementary building blocks out of which by various operations, the sentence is constructed. Since the kernel sentences underlying a given utterance seem, in a way, to incorporate the basic content of the utterance, such analysis also seems to suggest a means for investigating the organization of connected discourse, a task which has hitherto been beyond the reach of linguistic analysis.[10]

Before discussing what these passages say and do not say about kernel sentences, there are several comments that must be made. One of the grammatical devices currently employed by people active in the field of MT, linguistic analysis, and the design of thinking machines is the elimination of the subjunctive mood of verbs. It is simply not true that Chomsky has carried out a detailed study of English structure, nor has he found that its grammar can be greatly simplified. He should have used the subjunctive condition contrary to fact: "If we were to carry out . . . we would find. . . ." Then it would be recognized by his readers that he was stating only a prediction and that he had not conducted the investigation upon which his conclusions are supposedly based. It can be remarked parenthetically that all the great mechanical brains, translating machines, learning-machines, chess-playing machines, perceiving machines, etc., accounts of which fill our press, owe their "reality" to a failure to use the subjunctive mood. The game is played as follows: First, it is asserted that except for trivial engineering details, a program for a machine is equivalent to a machine. The flow chart for a program is equated to a program. And finally, the statement that a flow chart could be written for a nonexistent program for a nonexistent machine establishes the existence of the machine. In just this way Uttley's "Conditioned Reflex Machine," Rosenblatt's "Perceptron," Simon, Shaw, and Newell's "General Problem Solver," and many other nonexistent devices have been named in the literature and are referred to as though they existed.

Let us assume that Chomsky has found something and is not merely predicting what he would find if he had actually carried out a detailed study of English structure. What, exactly, has he found? Since it is certainly reasonable to ask that a mathematical or formal analysis of grammar be rigorous, it is by the same token reasonable to object to such descriptions of kernel sentences as:

(1) "A very small set . . . (in fact, probably finite)"
(2) "By and large meaning-preserving"
(3) "In some sense, the elementary 'content elements'"
(4) "Seem, in a way, to incorporate the basic content."

With reference to (1), something which is "probably finite" is at least "possibly infinite," which changes (1) to "a very small set . . . (in fact, possibly infinite)." As a matter of fact, it is demonstrable that simple declarative sentences in the English language constitute an infinite class, *e.g.*, the set of sentences: "2 follows 1." "3 follows 2." "4 follows 3," etc. Chomsky might amend his position here to say that he meant there is only a "small (probably finite, possibly infinite) set of types of kernel sentences." Unfortunately for this emendation it merely adds to the difficulty of describing the class K, the requirement of describing the classes $K_1, K_2, K_3 \ldots K_n$.

With reference to (2), there is certainly difficulty in determining what is meant by "by and large." Presumably anything which is "by and large meaning-preserving" is also "meaning changing." This is not a quibble. If Chomsky means that the meaning of kernels is invariant under transformation, he should say so and not fudge. As a matter of fact, he doesn't say so because such a statement would be clearly false and would be immediately recognized as such by the careful reader.

Statement (3) is a little more difficult to make clear. It might mean that "in some other sense kernel sentences are not content elements" or "in some sense something other than kernel sentences are content elements." Whichever interpretation is chosen, it is apparent that there is forthcoming no clear description of what a kernel sentence is.

Finally, (4) seems, in a way, to be saying something, but exactly what it seems to be saying, "in a way," is not very clear.

It is admitted that questions about language are difficult and that a careful writer is justified in using phrases like "seems," "in a way," "by and large," "in some sense," and "probably finite" in *speculations* about language, or even in ordinary descriptions of the grammar of a language; but such expressions have no place in what is supposedly a formal theory of grammar and linguistic transformations, and they leave the crucial notion of kernel sentence in an amorphous mess.

It might be said at this point that Chomsky doesn't define kernel sentences because the notion is a commonplace of logical and linguistic analysis; just as he doesn't define transformation since its meaning is well known to mathematicians. Unfortunately, the term "kernel" appears to be unique to Harris, Chomsky, and perhaps other students of Harris's work; hence, it is necessary to consider below what Harris has to say about kernels. However, it is probably true that Chomsky and Harris use the word "kernel" to suggest something like an atomic sentence or an atomic formula in logic.

Hence, the usage and/or meaning of "atomic formula" and "atomic sentence" in logic should be explored to see if Chomsky and Harris's work can stand with an undefined notion of "kernel."

Whether he invented it or not, it is certainly true that Ludwig Wittgenstein popularized the concept of atomic sentences among logicians and logical positivists. Wittgenstein advanced the view that all complex sentences are truth functions and hence either tautologous or contradictory transformations of simple, *i.e.*, atomic, sentences. The notion of atomic sentence is required to give an empirical, as opposed to a formal, content to discourse. (Note the similarity here to "elementary content elements.") An atomic sentence, said Wittgenstein, "agreed" with the facts, mapped the facts, or expressed the facts. An atomic sentence had no parts which were sentences. And, finally, an atomic sentence was true if what it said "was the case" and false if what it said "wasn't the case." The requirement that atomic sentences be true or false carried with it the requirement that they be "declarative." A question, a command, or evocation might be shorter and simpler than a declarative sentence, but since no statement of this type can have a truth value, they are eliminated from the class of atomic sentences. There is nothing in Chomsky's or Harris's studies that indicates that kernel sentences must have truth values. Hence, there is no reason why they should be declarative in the sense that Wittgenstein's atomic sentences are declarative. So far as length, simplicity, or the primitive character of meaning is concerned, there is not the slightest reason presented by Chomsky, Harris, or even by Wittgenstein against the view that evocations, commands, or questions, to say nothing of passives and subjunctives, cannot be regarded as kernel sentences with declarative sentences considered as transformations of whichever type is chosen as "elementary."

As a matter of fact, the notion of atomic sentence has almost disappeared from logical work. The term does not appear in the indexes to Quine's *Methods of Logic* nor Church's *Introduction to Mathematical Logic*. In his *Mathematical Logic*, Quine states that there are atomic logical formulae but no atomic logical statements. Church discusses "singulary" forms as forms having one free variable; from this it does not follow that a singulary form is also an atomic formula, since a singulary form with one free variable might contain more than one atomic formula; nor is every atomic logical formula singulary. For example, $x\epsilon y$ is an atomic formula having two variables. Although Quine denies that there are atomic logical statements, it might still be true that there are atomic statements; but being concerned with logic and not with metaphysics, as was Wittgenstein, Quine doesn't discuss them.

Rudolf Carnap discusses atomic sentences, which he defines as follows: "A sentence consisting of a predicate of degree n followed by n individual constants is called an atomic sentence." [11] This permits quite complicated atomic sentences and requires a supplementary definition of "simplest atomic sentences," namely, sentences consisting of one predicate followed by one individual constant. But Carnap, too, because he is interested in truth values, equates sentence with declarative sentence, a procedure not *prima facie* required for structural linguistics.

There is no reason to explore further the role of atomic formulae or atomic sentences in logic. It seems clear that logic is required to posit atomic formulae which contain no other formulae as parts in order to proceed with the quantification and truth functional composition of such formulae. There is no similar empirical or formal requirement for atomic sentences in ordinary discourse.

Even if there were such a requirement, it would not be met by the supposition of kernel sentences, because the essential characteristic of an atomic formula or an atomic sentence in logical discourse is that atomic formulae contain no formulae as parts and that atomic sentences contain no sentences as parts. But Harris is quite specific on the point that a "kernel" can include adjuncts which are "kernels," and that how far transformations are carried out is arbitrary:

> If we can find that certain transformations are responsible for separating out (into different kernels) items that we would like to keep together, we would omit these transformations and the regular application of the remaining transformations would give us kernels closer to the size and type we want.[12]

and

> If the adjunct contains . . . words which are centers in other kernels that adjunct is transformed into a separate kernel; otherwise it is not.[13]

It is recognized that on the matter of whether or not kernel sentences possess kernels, or potential kernels under transformation, as parts, there is undoubtedly disagreement between Harris and Chomsky. But this means that neither was justified in omitting a careful description of kernel sentences and that their conclusions are baseless in the absence of such descriptions.

There is one additional point which must be considered before kernel sentences and linguistic transformations can be dismissed categorically as scientific aberrations such as the influence of planets in astrology or the cranial bumps in phrenology. It may be supposed that it is possible to build a structure of linguistic operations upon an undefined primitive "kernel sentence." A parallel may be sought between such a view and the fact that operations in arithmetic are possible even if the nature of numbers remains unspecified; and the fact that logic can be developed even though considerable doubt remains concerning the nature of propositions. Unfortunately, the parallel breaks down because arithmetic and propositional logic are concerned with the relationships between numbers and propositions, respectively, and not with the internal nature of numbers or propositions. On the contrary, linguistic transformations are not concerned with the relations of undefined kernels to one another, but with internal modification of kernels themselves. In other words, transformational analysis necessarily requires a theory of kernel structure, whereas propositional calculus does not require a theory of the internal structure of propositions. Apparently Harris considered and rejected the crutch such a parallel might provide: "This [transformations of the same kernel] . . . is not the same as a reduction of English sentences to their logical equivalents. The tools of logic are not sufficient for a representation of the statements and problems of science."[14] Whatever such a statement may mean, it is appropriate as an epitaph for the science of linguistic transformations.

Bar-Hillel attempts to rescue Chomsky's doctrine of "kernel sentences" by throwing Harris to the wolves:

Chomsky, who is a former pupil of Harris and heavily indebted to him for many terms and underlying ideas, later came to use these terms in senses which were quite different from those given to them by Harris. More strictly, whereas with Chomsky terms like transformation or kernel have pretty well determined senses, their vagueness not exceeding the usual range adhering to almost all scientific terms, they are not at all well-defined with Harris, and with him rely for their meaning on some far-fetched and under-developed analogy with the use of these terms in modern abstract algebra.[15]

Both Bar-Hillel and Chomsky should be worried that their youthful agility, their ability to play fast and loose with words, and to use "no more than ordinarily vague terms" in logical and mathematical discussions, will someday catch up with them (even if in this book we have not already done so). A new generation of young Turks will appear and they will, in turn, lighten their baggage by throwing Chomsky and Bar-Hillel to the wolves.

If Chomsky and Harris represented a unique phenomenon, the amount of space devoted to this analysis of their views would not be justified. But the aberration they represent is widespread and has cast a mystique over the whole field of MT and related activities of machine handling of information. This mystique can be traced in the descriptions of recent activities of a number of organizations which appear in the volumes, *Current Research and Development in Scientific Documentation*,[16] issued by the National Science Foundation. One organization is engaged in "normalizing expressions without altering significantly their informative meaning." [17] A second is searching for "normalized English and has found [note the verb form] an algebraic representation of syntax which covers a large sub-class of English sentences." [18] A third conducts experiments in "automatic analysis of the syntactic structure of English sentences" and has let contracts "for research in the analysis of natural and artificial languages." [19] A fourth has designed an artificial language "intended as a flux for research activity . . . in the thesaurus

Linguistic Analysis 67

spirit."[20] A fifth is developing a "Metalanguage called Ruly English primarily descriptive of interrelational concepts."[21] A sixth is investigating "the range of useful relationships or functions of individual words and phrases" and has reported that "work on automatic coding of English or foreign language abstracts into machine language (with automatic interpretation to any other language)"[22] is well advanced. A seventh has "discovered patterns of relationships . . . [which extend] the language models described by Chomsky to cover 'grammars in generalized languages.' "[23] An eighth "is concerned with automatic programming and machine algorithm-synthesizing processes."[24] A ninth is developing lattices "the elements of which are semantic fields."[25] A tenth is approaching completion of a system which "will enable the automatic conversion of English canonical forms into appropriate inflected forms for the synthesis of English sentences at the output of an automatic translator."[26] An eleventh states that new techniques of analysis provide a "reasonable hope in the distant future to be able to program a machine to teach itself to translate."[27] And a twelfth investigated the theory of linguistic models and "was able to prove a series of basic theorems—among them some that were rather unexpected . . ."[28] And from this last of a dozen comes the closing text of this chapter: Any theorems about linguistic models would be unexpected, not to say impossible.

6 MAN-MACHINE RELATIONS

Several years ago, the Office of Naval Research inaugurated a program, known as ANIP (Army-Navy Instrumentation Program) for the redesign of airplane cockpits. There have been many such programs, but what distinguished this one was a radical (in the root sense of basic) approach to the problem of man-machine relationships. The general account of this program and its accomplishments are contained elsewhere.[1] This chapter will be concerned only with its concept of man-machine relationships and the light which this concept sheds on the validity of the endeavors to design machines to simulate the behavior of the human brain. It will be shown that the proper man-machine relation is one of complementation and augmentation, not simulation.

The human organism and its brain respond consciously to limited spectra of the world of radiation in which they function. Hence it is theoretically and practically important to design receptors and processors which can react to and derive information from portions of the radiation spectra to which the human organism is insensible. When this type of information has a steady or predictable character, and constitutes the total data for action, the machine can be programmed to respond to it by taking suitable action. If the information processed by the machine must be integrated with actions in ways which are unpredictable, then the ma-

Man-Machine Relations 69

chine function terminates in a display to which a human brain can react. The complex man-machine relationships of complementation, substitution, and augmentation are not varieties of simulation, and it will be shown that recent speculation concerning the simulation of human brains by machines is devoid of interest and does not contribute to a fruitful understanding of man-machine relationships.

If a machine is to simulate the behavior of a human brain, the designer of the machine must have a good notion of the behavior which is being simulated. That is to say, it is an initial requirement that any such enterprise specify as exactly and as completely as possible those activities or functions of the brain which are to be simulated, imitated, or even surpassed. It is unfortunately true that much of the theoretical and experimental work in this field has neglected this requirement and consequently has found itself mired in the classical vicious circle:

(1) A machine is proposed or constructed to simulate the human brain which is not described.
(2) The characteristics of the machine which are carefully described are then stated to be analogous to the characteristics of the brain.
(3) It is then "discovered" that the machine behaves like a brain. The circularity[2] consists in "discovering" what has already been posited.

To avoid this circularity, it is necessary to begin with some concept of the brain's activities or some definition of its functions. Such a definition can then provide an empirical measure of the degree to which any machine simulation of the brain is successful.

However, it must be recognized that it is not a simple matter to describe either the structure or function of the brain in such a way as to establish a standard of activities which are to be imitated or surpassed by a machine. And it is at this point that some help can be derived from the basic notions of the ANIP program. Much simplified, these notions can be stated as follows: For the first twenty-odd years of his life an airplane pilot grows up in an earth-bound environment. The organs which convey messages to his brain and the brain itself are biologically specialized to function in such an environment. Of even greater significance is the fact that these organs evolved through millions of years by a process of natural selection to perform certain activities necessary for the survival of the species man in its natural environment.

If this pilot is taken ten miles into space and propelled through space at speeds of one thousand miles an hour or more, he finds himself in an unfamiliar and biologically unsuitable environment. His sense organs no longer pick up the significant stimuli; and what are picked up convey little or no useful information to his brain. Under such circumstances, the pilot is at first supplied with instruments; but as the number and variety of such instruments multiply and the pilot is called upon for faster and faster reaction speeds, the environment of instruments also becomes unsuitable for the proper functioning of the brain and its sensors. Something can be done at this point by attempting to re-train the pilot; that is, to overcome and modify the environmental adjustments of his first twenty years. But training which is designed to overcome several million years of evolutionary adjustment does not afford a very hopeful prospect.

There is, however, another method, namely, the use of "sensors" and "instruments" to create or simulate in the cockpit an environment which is suitable for the biological organism it contains.

Man-Machine Relations 71

Consider the case of a man entering a dark room or a cave. If the man could train himself to orient himself and move around by picking up infrared, acoustic, and radio waves, he could function in such an environment; but how much simpler it is to turn on the lights and thus create a natural environment for the awake biological organism. It might be possible to train chickens not to sleep but to lay eggs in the dark; however, it is much simpler to provide light artificially so the chickens will continue their normal daylight function in a "daylight" environment.

From these considerations it is possible to derive a fairly simple and straightforward functional definition of the brain: The brain is that organ of the body which processes information received from a relatively stable environment (including the body itself) in order to secure successful behavior of the organism in relation to its environment. More concretely, the eye which conveys certain information to the brain enables the brain to distinguish between an open door and a closed door, so that in one case we walk through, and in the other we stop before bumping our noses.

The essential character of this definition is that it recognizes the pragmatic, biological character of the brain. It is to be sharply distinguished from any definition or description of the brain which neglects biological function or considers it a minor characteristic of a nonbiological entity. For example, a clinical thermometer is used in a biological environment but it is not usually considered to be a biological organism. A computer may also be used in a biological environment without thereby becoming a biological organism.

It is true that a biological organism will have other characteristics which can be characterized as mechanical, physical, chemical, electrical, or even logical; but by emphasizing the brain's role in the adaptation and survival of the organism and species, the problem of "simulation" of the brain by a machine is set in a new perspective, at least a perspective which is almost uniformly ignored by the coterie of computer enthusiasts.

The term "simulation" which is encountered in man-machine discussions is almost as troublesome as the term "brain." "Simulation" obviously admits of degree; more importantly, it may be partial or abstract. For example, a pound of cheese can be simulated by placing a pound piece of metal opposite on a scale. That is, the weight of the cheese is simulated but not its flavor, aroma, or nutritive properties. It may be argued that the weight is the "essential" character of the cheese and that when the weight has been simulated all other properties may be regarded as trivia.

It is unfortunately true that most of the literature on the simulation of brains by machines partakes of this character. An author selects one characteristic of the brain (or sometimes even posits one) which he regards as essential. He then points out that his machine can simulate the characteristic he has selected. It is reasonable to suspect that the choice of brain characteristic to be simulated is motivated by a prior knowledge of what the machine can do—and again the cozy but vicious circle is established.

One may wonder why reputable scientific journals publish material of this sort and why it should have an audience beyond the readers of the Sunday supplements. The answer to this question will be presented below. But it is necessary in the first instance to establish the basic importance of the above definition by subjecting it to an examination within the context of some formal discussion of brain simulation. The problem here is to select some formal discussion which can

Man-Machine Relations   73

be considered both typical and representative of the highest level yet attained by discussions of the subject.

At the 1955 Institute of Radio Engineers National Convention, the Professional Group on Electronic Computers sponsored a symposium on "The Design of Machines to Simulate the Behavior of the Human Brain." The panel members represented the top echelon of workers in this field and it can be presumed that in this symposium most, if not all, of the crucial issues of simulation were introduced. In any case this symposium will be accepted as representing "the state of the art" or the "state of thinking" on the topic of machine simulation of brains, and most subsequent references will be to this text.

One of the first points made clear in the symposium was that a distinction must be made between simulation of structure and simulation of function.[3] Furthermore, once this distinction had been made, the participants came to fairly general agreement that computers could not be considered structurally similar to human brains, and that the simulation of brain structure by a machine structure is not a very promising enterprise. In fact, after Dr. O. H. Schmitt, the neurophysiologist on the panel, noted that:

In all probability the central nervous system including its memory and computing functions is a widely distributive statistical time-place-state system where memory of a particular event is smeared out over some millions of cells and these same cells simultaneously hold many millions of other memory traces.[4]

Dr. Minsky commented that "no one seems to have been able to [build or suggest a model to] indicate how such a thing might work."[5] Even earlier in the discussion Dr. A. G. Oettinger noted that "many machines of the future will continue to have only a functional resemblance to living organisms."[6]

And Dr. M. E. Maron suggested that "only similarity of inputs and outputs be considered and that computers or brains be looked upon as 'black boxes' which might have no similarity of structure or components." [7]

It is true, as Dr. Schmitt indicated, that some computer enthusiasts have looked for structural analogs between the wire networks of electronic computers and the nerve networks of living organisms, and have made much of the fact that nerve impulses seem to be "electrical" in character. But Turing has noted that:

> The fact that Babbage's Analytical Engine was to be entirely mechanical will help us to rid ourselves of a superstition. Importance is often attached to the fact that modern digital computers are electrical, and that the nervous system also is electrical. Since Babbage's machine was not electrical, and since all digital computers are in a sense equivalent, we see that this use of electricity cannot be of theoretical importance.[8]

It seems, then, that we may dispense with "structural" simulation—with Frankensteins, robots, and the whole phantasmagoria of artificial men made out of artificial protoplasm, and confine our attention to simulation of function; but here we note a general hiatus in the symposium. While everyone seemed to agree that the interesting and important kind of simulation is simulation of function, there was no discussion or attempt to specify the functions which are to be simulated.

It certainly does not make much sense to say that the function of the brain is to play chess or translate languages and that chess playing machines and translation machines are thereby successful simulations of the human brain. Presumably, those machine designers or theorists who occupy themselves with chess playing and translation think of them as activities which illustrate some underlying functional competence in man, which competence is to be simulated by a machine. The competence which underlies such activities may be called thinking; and one may then say that the function of the brain is thinking and that a mechanical thinking machine simulates the function of the brain. But this too is nonsense—the brain doesn't think any more than lungs breathe—it is man which does both. Furthermore, in the same sense that the brain thinks, it perceives, wills, feels, imagines, hates, loves, etc. Is the machine simulation of the brain also to cover these functions?

In short, to define the brain by attributing to it the function of "thinking" is merely to state a problem. How do we recognize thinking and how do we know that any given brain or machine is thinking? This is not a specious nor captious question. At the third London Conference on Information Theory, one of the participants stated his position as follows:

We may refer the question "Can a machine induce?" to the general question "Can a machine do what a man does when he says he is thinking?" The affirmative answer offered by the Italian Operational School to either question should then be connected with the last (and not with the first) of the following four combinations (a) man thinks, machines think; (b) man thinks, machines do not think; (c) man does not think, machines think; (d) man does not think, machines do not think.[9]

Here is simulation of function with a vengeance; according to behavioristic or positivistic metaphysics, nothing thinks—men just move as determined by their inputs—and a machine can perhaps be built to simulate any described movement of the human body.

The simulation of men by machines based upon their like inability to think is a kind of metaphysical nonsense which has been noted earlier. A large part of the acceptance, or patience, which is exhibited towards the literature of machine simulation of the human brain can be attributed to a cultural lag, the fact that the mechanistic, materialistic philosophy of the nineteenth century is today's "common sense." If, ultimately, man is nothing but a machine, in the sense in which Descartes thought animals to be machines (Descartes exempted man from mechanism on theological grounds), then the simulation of human brains by machines can be interpreted as the simulation of a machine by a machine.

It is a curious fact of intellectual history that years after the complete abandonment of materialism and determinism in physics there should be a revival of these doctrines with reference to human action. Late in the nineteenth century, Ernst Heinrich Haeckel's *Riddle of the Universe* was a best-seller. It purported to give a materialistic account of the universe based upon concepts of Newtonian physics. Developments in physical theory ended Haeckel's popularity and significance. But every real advance in science is apt to bring with it a chorus of interpreters which tells us, "Now, at last, the riddle of the universe is solved. Yesterday, we thought that man was 'nothing but' atoms in motion; now we know he is 'nothing but' a highly complex digital computer." It is worth noting that the men who make the real contribution to scientific advancement rarely become "nothing but-ers." Bush and Von Neumann, who developed the modern computer technology, do not overstate the analogy between men and machines; but many of their followers at Massachusetts Institute of Technology and elsewhere have little restraint in this regard.

There is a remarkable symmetry in the fact that Alfred North Whitehead, after a half century of concern with mathematics, logic, and physical theory, came out with a philosophy of organism expressed in essentially biological categories, and that Von Neumann, considering the general logic of automata, concludes that "it may be that logic will have to undergo a pseudomorphosis to neurology to a much greater extent than the reverse." [10]

It is certainly more desirable to avoid metaphysical controversy on this topic and to accept the *prima facie* distinction between machines and living organisms. In any case, when the computer theorist refuses to accept the empirical account of the biological function of the brain and takes refuge in materialistic metaphysics because he cannot state how machines are to simulate such a function, he exhibits a kind of inverted fundamentalism which is impregnable because it is so dogmatically ignorant.

It can now be seen why the pragmatic definition of the function of the brain in biological terms has a therapeutic value. To simulate the functions of the brain by a machine, is to make a machine which processes information in order to secure the survival of a biological organism of which it is an integral part, not to mention the species to which the biological organism belongs. Until someone has some specific ideas about how to build a machine of this type, it seems advisable to stop talking about mechanical simulation of the human brain.

We may return, at this point, to the notion of man-machine relationships introduced in the opening paragraphs of this chapter. Once the barren notion of simulation is eliminated, it becomes possible to investigate the truly important question, namely, how the machine may extend the function of the brain by processing and transforming information which cannot be handled by the brain so that the brain can handle it. This is another way of saying that machines can convert an environment in which the brain cannot function into one in which it can function. (It is appropriate to note that the word "simulation" first entered into the machine picture with reference to the use of a machine to simulate the special conditions of an airplane considered as the environment of a pilot, as in a Link trainer.) Consider again the simple case of a thermometer. The brain and its senses lack the ability to measure exactly the rate of thermal radiation. Hence, its own judgments of hot and cold are apt to be quite vague and confined both to narrow limits and to large intermediate jumps. The thermometer, on the other hand, can respond to thermal radiation by changing the arrangement of the light rays reflected from it. The brain can react very specifically to these light rays, which it processes to arrive at the perception of the coincidence of a line of color with a row of numbers. The essential fact here is that the machine handles messages which the brain cannot.

The role of the thermometer (in this example a clinical thermometer) may be extended by eliminating the numbers on it and substituting a series of phrases at appropriate intervals: Go to work; Rest; Go to bed; Call a doctor; Call an ambulance. It might even be possible to connect sensors to the thermometer which would convert a particular reading to the manipulation of a telephone dial to call the doctor. But if the high reading on the thermometer were attributable to a vaccination then the programmed behavior would be wrong. At this point a human brain would be required to integrate all the information in the environment in terms of the special experiences and purposes of the human organism.

Another simple illustration can be drawn in terms of a man sitting in a room in which he is aware, within certain narrow limits, of thermal radiation, acoustical radiation, and optical radiation. He is surrounded, of course, by radiation to which he is insensible. At a certain time a radio is introduced into the room, or more spectacularly, a television set. The television set is a device which can convert radiation, to which the human organism does not consciously respond, into familiar sights and sounds to which it can and does respond. Because broadcasting would not occur if there were no radios or television sets, we sometimes talk as though broadcasting were a process of sending messages to a receiver; and we assume that the messages would not be in the environment if the receivers weren't present. Actually, the messages are in the environment. We are at all times enveloped in radiation—to which we are insensible—from all over the earth, from heavenly bodies, and from the very walls around us.

Here, then, is a meaningful task for machine builders with an understanding of the function of the human brain and the function of machines in the man-machine relationship. The brain and its senses are highly specialized for the purpose of survival in an environment with limited variability. We wish to enable man to function high in space, in the depths of the sea, when he moves at tremendous speeds, when he is encased in an armored tank, etc. Under such circumstances the messages the brain receives from its environment cease to convey information of value, that is, information in terms of which the man can insure his survival and carry out his purposes. A man so placed is desperately dependent on machines to convert the unfamiliar to the familiar; to respond to radiation from distant objects before they can be picked up by human senses; to utilize radiation bands beyond the limited human range in order to derive information about the environment; and to process such information into a form which the man finds familiar and meaningful.

7   MAN-MACHINE RELATIONS
IN DEFENSE SYSTEMS

The statement that man is "nothing but" a digital computer may be not only bad metaphysics and of dubious scientific or heuristic validity, but also may be dangerously false. This is so because today such statements are intended for more than philosophic or scientific debate. They are made to influence the allocation of research funds and defense budgets and to guide defense planning. Hence, their uncritical acceptance can lead to catastrophe. It is in the context of such considerations that the following is presented. It will be shown, for example, that the research effort, directed toward fully automatic defense systems, rests on a number of specific conclusions regarding the nature of living organisms and the simulation [1] of such organisms by machines. In examining the evidence for these conclusions, it is necessary to refer again to a topic treated earlier, namely, the notion of possibility as a guide to research and the reasonableness of distinguishing between the possible and the impossible as goals of scientific research. We shall also explore two quite technical questions which may appear to be remote from the theoretical problems of man-machine relations and the practical problems of automating defense systems, namely:

Defense Systems   81

(1) What are the meanings of "identity" and "similarity" as relations which underlie scientific inductions and the formulation of general concepts?

(2) What is the role of consciousness in living organisms?

In 1958, *Business Week* analyzed numerous unsuccessful business and government applications of computers.[2] In most cases, the failures were failures in detail—failures of large systems concepts to pay off in detailed accomplishment. That is why in considering the problem of man-machine relations it is necessary to go beyond speculation and aphorisms and to be concerned with detailed physiological accounts of human perception and action. It has been held that the wide gap between the promise and performance of thinking machines is a mere matter of "engineering detail." A measure of the problem of "engineering detail" can be found in the history of mechanical translation, which, as has been shown, presents a record of glowing prognostications about what is possible and a record of actual failure in accomplishment. There is a growing realization that even approximate mechanical translation may be impractical just because there are too many engineering details; that is, a computer handling 10^6 or 10^7 bits per second may be no match for the human translator's intuitive recognition of a meaning. Similar considerations seem to limit chess-playing machines to "a-few-move" games of a small selection of pieces.

When the focus of interest turns from relatively controlled problems, such as mechanical translation or chess playing, to defense systems and strategies, the gap between the promise of complete automation and its accomplishment becomes even wider. There are reasons to expect that this gap will be narrowed; but the narrowing may be a result of more detailed knowledge and better understanding of men and machines, rather than a naïve effort to automate human decision and creativity.

In the design and development of large systems, whether weapon systems, communication systems, intelligence systems, data processing systems, etc., the systems engineer must consider those spatial and temporal positions at which an interaction takes place between an operator and a device. The importance of this interaction is evident in the recent growth of human engineering as a special synthesis of psychology and engineering. The human operator reacts to information presented to him by a device, and his reaction may include decision processes and the exercise of controls to guide subsequent phases of the machine's operation. The manner in which the operator reacts to the responses, and the probability of error in both comprehension and response, have become the concern of the psychologist in human engineering; whereas the engineer must consider the factors made known to him by the psychologist in designing his display panels, handles, control knobs, etc.

The existence of systems compatibility problems between men and machines has led to both practical and speculative effort designed to increase the automation of systems by decreasing human interposition. Full automation of a process or system seems a desirable goal; and it is generally felt that, in principle—if not in practice, as defined by the "state of the art" at a given moment of time—full automation is quicker, cheaper, more reliable, and more productive than a semiautomatic man-machine system. It is in this sense that the guided missile rather than the piloted aircraft is looked upon as the ultimate weapon. Similarly, this assumption has led to concepts of defense and attack systems in which computers and robots on one side war with computers and robots on the other. Presumably, the human exists to express his purposes by pushing the first button, and to enjoy the fruits of victory or to suffer the penalties of defeat. But this presumption might also be questioned; in fact, it has been questioned by those who envision decision-making machines, having creative abilities. Such machines might make their own decisions concerning the appropriateness of going to war and might even learn to enjoy or suffer the results of their actions.

These considerations are not fanciful. They are intended to elicit the recognition that unless the human being is ready to abdicate, to be replaced in entirety by a machine, automation can never be total. At some point, if only at the beginning and end of a machine process, there will be a problem of man-machine relationships.

If automation can never be total, then the "where", "how much," and "when" of human interposition must be understood as questions of degree. Further, there should be discoverable principles in terms of which the degree of human interposition and the degree of automation for maximizing the result and minimizing the investment in any specific system can be determined.

The general view that increased automaticity and decreased human participation in systems is *always* desirable is here being denied. It will be shown that this doctrine is not only false but that it may have deleterious effects on our national defense. It will be shown further that this doctrine has its origin in a naïve and superficial concept of both machine capability and human nature. Speculation about "thinking machines" is in itself a harmless exercise and has been indulged in since the time Lucretius described the mind and thinking as composed of tiny, round, small atoms which moved very rapidly, as compared to the heavier, slower moving corporeal atoms. However, when such speculation ceases to be a metaphysical exercise and becomes a guiding principle of a major segment of the defense effort, it is serious enough to warrant detailed examination. Out of this examination, there should emerge serious and not fanciful concepts of the role of man and machine in any man-machine system. The view being advanced here, in contradistinction to the prevalent view, is that there are radical and basic discontinuities between digital computers and living organisms; that the essential characteristics of living organisms cannot be simulated, copied, imitated, or surpassed by machines. It is also true that the essential characteristics of machines cannot be profitably copied, simulated, or imitated by living organisms.

Unless one has carefully followed the literature being produced by some of the major laboratories concerned with computers and their development, it is perhaps difficult to realize how prevalent has become the doctrine of man-machine identity. Not only are serious technical journals full of articles on thinking-machines, learning-machines, perceiving-machines, decision-making machines, and the like, but even the popular press has learned to follow the fashion and to report on such marvels without even the faintest suggestions of tongue-in-cheek. It appears that the "sputnik," as the latest practical realization of Buck Rogers's speculations, has made it unfashionable to think that anything is impossible or even impractical. Today, it is the mark of sound scientific perspective to accept the wildest speculation as describing tomorrow's operating gadget. Thus, *Time* [3] in reporting on an international conference on "The Mechanization of Thought Processes" held at Britain's National

Defense Systems   85

Physical Laboratory, noted that Dr. Minsky, a representative of Massachusetts Institute of Technology, "felt that the problem is unduly complicated by irrational human reverence for human intelligence. . . . Dr. Minsky is convinced that there is nothing special about intelligence or creativity." During the same week, *The New Yorker*[4] reported on an interview with Dr. Frank Rosenblatt, the designer of the *Perceptron,* a machine which demonstrates that "a non-biological organism will achieve an organization of its environment in a meaningful way . . . our machine (is) a self-organizing system (and) that's precisely what any brain is."

And once again we can add to these sources a passage from our favorite scholarly (*sic*) work, the *Automata Studies:*

> Human beings learn, they remember, and their behavior is modified by experience in various ways. They ingeniously solve problems, compose symphonies, create works of art and literature and engineering, and pursue various goals. They seem to exhibit extremely complex behavior. . . . In this section, we will describe a general method for designing robots with any specified behavioral properties whatsoever. They can be designed to do *any* desired physically possible thing under any given circumstance and past experience, and certainly any naturally given "robot" such as Smith or Jones can do no more.[5]

In examining the existing literature to discover the reasons for this inordinate optimism concerning what digital computers and similar machines may one day accomplish, one is struck by the paucity of real evidence and accomplishment. Most of it reads like exercises in imaginative extrapolation. Von Neumann has considered this process of imaginative extrapolation and found it completely unwarranted in fact and in logic;[6] but his warnings have, in general, been unheeded. The prevalent notion that nothing is impossible in science seems to justify the most extreme claims of wonders to come; and the more extreme, the better.[7]

It is perhaps worthwhile to point out that many of the truly momentous scientific advances have been demonstrations that certain things are impossible—that certain lines of investigation are sterile and can lead to no significant results. From the second law of thermodynamics, the *impossibility* of perpetual-motion machines can be demonstrated; from the Heisenberg principle of indeterminism, the *impossibility* of determining the exact position and velocity of an electron can be deduced; from the theory of relativity, the *impossibility* of determining simultaneity at different places can be deduced; and Goedel's theorem holds that it is *impossible* to state a set of axioms of arithmetic that is both complete and consistent. Goedel's theorem has a direct bearing on the limitations of computers which have been noted by Turing, Church, Nagel and others; although these limitations, like those pointed out by Von Neumann, have been, in general, overlooked.

Certainly the notion of impossibility, when used rigorously, should be restricted to formal systems in which it can be equated to contradiction. The impossibilities, which have been noted above, are formal in the sense that they are deducible from accepted general propositions and definitions and are not matters of pure empirical observations. By the same token, much of the discussion of machine *possibilities* is purely semantical. As we have seen, "learning" is defined as a set of mechanical activities; then it is determined that machines can "learn." Similarly, proofs by definition have become current in discussing and "discovering" analogous components and functions in living brains and computers. But the acceptance of certain basic definitions of machines and their functions may be crucial in justifying or eliminating large research projects. Among such basic definitions are found the deceptively simple (actually, most difficult) notions of "identity" and "similarity."

It is possible to explain "similarity" in terms of "identity"; it is also possible to explain "identity" in terms of "similarity." Which term is taken as basic and undefined, a matter which is largely arbitrary, leads to the identification or a radical distinction between machine activities and thought processes. If "similarity" is defined in terms of "identity" and "difference," then a good case can be made for man-machine identity; on the other hand, if "identity" is defined in terms of "observed similarity," then a radical discontinuity must be posited between men and machines.

Suppose "similarity" is defined in terms of identity, considered as an understood or undefined term, as follows:
A is similar to B, means that with respect to a set of properties, $P_1, P_2, P_3, -P_n$,
  (1) Some members of the set, P_1-P_n, namely, P_1, P_2, P_3, are properties of A and not properties of B,
  (2) Some members of the set, P_1-P_n, namely, P_4, P_5, P_6, are properties of B and not properties of A,
  (3) Some members of the set, P_1-P_n, namely, P_7, P_8, P_9, are properties of A and properties of B.

If A is a distinct physical entity and does not include B and is not included in B, the sense in which both A and B can be characterized by identical properties occasions some difficulty. The brown of the chair and the brown of the table are not identical color patches. We seem faced here with the nominalistic alternative of regarding the word "brown" as a general term which applies to two distinct nonidentical

88 Defense Systems

color patches, in which case any nonverbal relationship of identity disappears; or we can accept the traditional realistic solution and regard brown as a universal, *i.e.*, a property which is always self-identical and independent of its exemplification at any time and place.[8] In this case, the brown of the table and the brown of the chair could be regarded as identical. The notion of identity seems to involve self-identity; that is, anything is identical only with itself and not with anything else. If the similarity of two objects is defined in terms of their identity and difference, there must be a self-identical property or properties which is/are shared by the two objects.

In the report of the device called the Perceptron, which is designed to recognize the similarity of images or stimuli, "similarity" is defined as follows:

> Consider a system in which the presentation of a visual image evokes activity in some set of cells, which might be scattered throughout the nervous system. If a second image evokes activity in exactly the same set of cells, it will be considered identical. . . . If the set of cells excited includes some members of the first set, the two images will be considered "similar" to a degree which varies with the proportion of excited cells which are common to the two stimuli.[9]

Here "similarity" is defined as a degree of identity; and the identity is self-identity, *i.e.*, the stimulation of the same cells. There may be difficulty in giving physical meaning to this definition. For example, it is unlikely that cells remain self-identical and unchanging through time, *i.e.*, through successive stimuli; and certainly there is no empirical evidence that observed similarities between colors and sounds (which may be called "bright" or "sombre") involve over-

Defense Systems 89

lapping sets of cells, either in the nervous system or the brain. But the definitions may be considered arbitrary; and certainly the designer of the Perceptron is justified in indicating what he means by "similarity" and "identity." It must also be recognized that this definition fits the assumption that all recognition of similarity can be digitalized and, therefore, mechanized.

The reduction of any operation to a program for a computer can be understood as a reduction to a set of identities and differences. The very concept of binary coding implies the reduction of a term, concept, operation, etc., to a set of identities and differences. All holes in a punched card are identical holes. To be sure, any one hole is physically distinct from another; but, any hole in contact with a reading element is considered identical with any other hole similarly positioned. The response of the reading head to a hole is presumed to be self-identical at all times. Hence, if it is assumed that any biological or human judgment of similarity can be exhaustively and completely analyzed into a set of identities and differences, then it may be further assumed that a machine can be constructed and programmed to match such recognition.

Suppose the process of definition is reversed and "similarity" is taken as the basic indefinable. The identity of any two items A and B can be defined as the possession of similar properties. Now a curious fact emerges. Whereas the human recognition seems simple, direct, and is, in fact, creative—as when we note the similarity between an impressionist painting, a poem of Mallarmé, and music by Debussy—no one has the faintest idea how to design or program a digital machine to recognize similarity; nor is it necessary to con-

90 *Defense Systems*

sider aesthetic experiences in noting the creative recognition of similarity. Such acts are performed constantly by decision makers in war, politics, and business.

If the statements relating the identity and similarity of stimuli to identical or overlapping sets of cells set forth in the discussion of the Perceptron are considered to be empirical statements rather than definitions, then it is reasonable to consider their truth or falsehood. As empirical statements, they would be asserting a real relation between the similarity of perceived stimuli and the overlapping of nerve cells. If such statements are true, it would follow that any two stimuli which did not stimulate overlapping sets of cells could not be similar to one another.

On this point, there exists strong, almost incontrovertible evidence that the similarity of stimuli does not involve the stimulation of overlapping or common nerve cells. Fifty years ago, Sherrington reported a remarkable series of experiments on binocular vision. These experiments involved the controlled stimulus of each retina to insure the exact similarity of stimuli; the stimuli to each retina were at times synchronous and at other times alternated at various controlled rates. The results of these experiments established in functional or physiological terms what seemed to be indicated anatomically; namely, that there is no common nerve path from the two retinae, and that binocular perception does not involve any spatial connection between nerve endings in the cortex. Sherrington's own conclusion, which he italicized to emphasize, follows:

Our experiments show, therefore, that during binocular regard of an objective image each uniocular mechanism develops independently a sensual image of considerable completeness. The singleness of the binocular perception results from union of these

Defense Systems 91

elaborated uniocular sensations. The singleness is therefore the product of a synthesis that works with already elaborated sensations contemporaneously proceeding. The cerebral seats of right-eye and left-eye visual images are thus shown to be separate.[10]

Forty years later, Sherrington repeated this conclusion and reemphasized its importance:

Congruent images from corresponding retinal points give one single image to the mind, a single mental image. This has often been taken as evidence of central conjunction of the nervous mechanism of the two retinal points . . . There is thus no evidence that the nervous paths from two corresponding retinal points, right and left, reach a common mechanism in the brain. The corresponding right eye and left eye perceptions are however contemporary. Their contemporaneity fuses them. There is here no need of spatial coupling in the brain.[11]

The Perceptron presumably recognizes similar shapes such as the following squares:

If the reader will look at either square with one eye and after a moment of time look at either square with the other eye, he will certainly experience and note the similarity of his perceptions. Yet this similarity does not, as a matter of fact, involve any common nervous mechanism or common meeting place in the brain of the two similar visual stimuli.

The significance of Sherrington's conclusions is not only that they establish the empirical falsity of the account of similarity in the description of the Perceptron but that they deal a devastating blow to the whole development of nerve-net theory as set forth in the original paper by McCulloch-Pitts and subsequent papers by Kleene, Von Neumann, Minsky, Culbertson, etc. Nerve-net theory represents the summation

92 Defense Systems

of inputs resulting in a single output as *always* involving spatial coupling of inputs. The inputs supposedly come together at the receptor, the synapse, or "the little black box." According to Sherrington, the union of inputs at a synapse is a false representation of the union of inputs which occurs in binocular vision. Hence, McCulloch-Pitts nets are not truly representative of nervous action, at least in the case of vision. It is also quite likely that there is a similar lack of spatial connection of nerves in the integration of sound heard with each ear. And most certainly there is no spatial or neural connection involved in unification of a visual and tactile stimulation which occurs when we attribute a visual and tactile stimulation to the same object. This analysis of identity and similarity and the concrete evidence supplied by physiology seem to establish scientifically that simple analogs between computer circuits and perceiving organisms are specious. It would seem to follow that any part of the defense effort which proceeds on the basis of making automata or robots which are structurally analogous to human organisms is scientifically unsound and has very dim prospects of success.

At this point, however, a new complication may be introduced into the man-machine problem. Although the designer of the Perceptron states that "the basic organization of the Perceptron is similar to that of a biological system," [12] it has been noted in the previous chapter that others who share his general position about the ability of machines have avoided the assertion of *structural* similarity or identity and have claimed only to be able to reproduce any function of the human mind with a suitably designed digital computer.

It has been pointed out that the wheel has no structural counterpart in animal organisms and yet performs mechanically a function performed by the limbs of animal organisms. Nevertheless, the notion of functional similarity or simulation is very vague and seems to involve the concept of purpose. A wheel has a functional similarity to limbs only in the sense that both serve similar human purposes. Apart from human purposes, a wheel has no purposes and no functions.

The concept of a machine which functions to serve *human purposes* is valid; and the issue which must be solved is simply the question as to whether any and all human purposes and human actions can be served by machines, cheaper, more effectively, and more reliably than they can be directly served by human actions. Although this issue is speculative, since no machines have been designed which are functionally identical with living organisms, many human activities have been replaced by devices of various kinds. And those who extrapolate on the basis of actual accomplishment seem to claim that given any specified function of a living organism, a machine can be built to perform that function (again the qualifications—cheaper, more effectively, more reliably, etc.—are to be understood). The substantiation or repudiation of such a claim is not a simple matter. The problem is not formal nor semantical, but factual. This means that the correct decision must rest upon an empirical study of the functions of living organisms; and upon a measure of the success of designing and building machines to carry out such functions. Even when the problem is narrowed by eliminating certain aesthetic and creative functions and limiting consideration to the functions of living organisms in defense activities, it remains extraordinarily difficult. Consider, for example, the function of conscious decision-making by a living organism. There exists very substantial evidence that the function of consciousness is to introduce novelty or nonpredictable decision-making into animal behavior as contrasted with reflex action, which proceeds on an unconscious level and seems to require no novel decisions, *i.e.*, is successfully carried out on an unconscious level. An argument for the functional replacement of such human action by a machine might take one of two paths. On one hand, it might be said that a machine could also introduce novelty and nonpredictable action (not as a random action, but as a purposeful solution not derivable from the programming of the machine). Such a notion involves the concept of purposeful machines guiding themselves and making conscious decisions not foreseen nor provided for by the machine designer. Presumably, the Perceptron is such a device; but the Perceptron does not exist except as a program in another device and it is certainly difficult, if not impossible, to understand how a computer program which consists of coding for a series of operations and instructions can establish how a Perceptron is to perform activities for which, in principle, neither programs nor instructions can be written.

The second and more usual argument for the functional replacement of humans by machines takes another path. It proceeds along behavioristic lines to deny any real function to consciousness; with consciousness eliminated, decision-making becomes a mathematically predictable action based on previously available data.

It is certainly true that many human actions are, and more should be, based upon a mathematical calculation of probabilities. When action is predictable and required on the basis of measurable or countable evidence, it seems reasonable to substitute machine control for human decision, especially if such probabilities can be calculated in a reason-

Defense Systems 95

able time and can provide a higher expectation of success than a nonquantitative intuitive judgment.

It can be seen that the aim of *fully* automatic warfare and defense involves several assumptions which may or may not be true, namely, that an unpredictable enemy action, that is, an action not provided for in the programming of a device, will never occur; that machine calculation of the best action will always be faster and more reliable than intuitive human judgment; that creative improvisation will never be required in a defense situation; and that generalization and the development of new concepts or the consideration of new possibilities for action are not required in defense planning or activity. Hence, the question of fully automatic warfare is not only a matter of speculation concerning what is or is not possible in the future, but depends upon the probable truth or falsity of certain assumptions being made in the present.

What sort of evidence would be required to establish such assumptions or to show that they are unwarranted? The enemy in warfare is not a missile nor a computer, but a man who directs missiles and designs computers. It is his action which must be predicted and countered with our missiles and computers. The problem is this: Can the action of a human enemy be programmed and predicted in our computers in a manner which will make human intervention and human judgment of desirable counter-measures unnecessary in our defense systems?

Since these assumptions are mainly concerned with human behavior, it seems reasonable to get the answers we require from physiologists rather than from computer designers or electrical engineers. If human functions are to be replaced by machines, the basic requirement is an understanding of human functions. Without evidence from the physiologist, at this point, the argument would revert to meaningless circularity. The electrical engineer tells us what his devices can do; he cannot tell us significantly that they can do whatever a human can do unless he describes human capability independently of his machines. If he defines human capability in terms of machine capability, he becomes guilty of the stupidest kind of question-begging.

It is safer to get from the physiologist a description of human functions; then the electrical engineer can tell us how he would build or design a machine to perform just those functions.

Careful physiologists like Sherrington and J. C. Eccles [13] insist that conscious psychical (*i.e.*, nonmechanical) integration of experience is a fact that has nonpredictable effects on human action. Here nonpredictable means nonpredictable in principle and not merely on the basis of our existing knowledge. Perhaps the word "creative," in spite of its theological overtones, is better than "nonpredictable," since the latter term is sometimes interpreted as a purely negative present fact about our knowledge; whereas the free action of consciousness is positive. There is no point in saying that, if we knew enough, conscious decision and action could be predicted. The point is, we do know enough to know that such a supposition is meaningless; just as it is meaningless to attempt to refute or overturn the positive insight of the Heisenberg principle of indeterminacy by supposing that, if we knew enough, determinism would be reintroduced into physics. We do know enough to know that behavior of electrons is indeterminate; that determinism as a physical theory is false. Similarly, we know enough to know that the role of consciousness is to introduce significant degrees of freedom and novelty into human activity.

It seems reasonable to assume that in any future defense situation, there will be a role for conscious human beings, but the extent of their role remains to be determined. And the final topic of this chapter will be a general suggestion for a method of making this determination.

Without any preconceived doctrines concerning how far automation may be expected to be valid, a series of defense problems ranging from the individual action of a pilot in his aircraft to a large-scale maneuver should be studied and analyzed. There will be considerable agreement that, at least in terms of the present state of the art, certain actions are obviously the kinds of things machines should perform and certain other actions seem to involve human judgment or similar human capability as opposed to machine capabilities. A detailed analysis of these areas of agreement should disclose certain generalized descriptions of actions which match machine capabilities. There will be a gray area, at least in the initial stages of the analysis, concerning which it will not be easy to determine whether automation is indicated. But if generally accepted criteria of machine action and human action emerge from the analysis of clearly marked-out aspects of a defense situation, these criteria can be used to reduce the gray area.

The implications of this type of procedure for defense planning are enormous. The development of practical automatic warfare involving defense and countermeasures can proceed forthwith in all areas in which such automation promises to be of real benefit. And there should be constant effort to discover, to abstract, and to automate all formal elements of decision processes involved in defense systems. None of the assumptions listed above is involved in such activities. On the other hand, the training of individuals and the development of experience and judgment concerning nonautomatic problems can also be expedited. Human engineering can come into its own, not as a study of human responses to dials, handles, and displays, but as a science of determining man-machine functions in a total systems concept.

8 MEANING AS A CONTINUUM

Throughout this book the common sense distinction between a symbol as a physical event in nature, *i.e.*, a shape or sound, and a symbol as a carrier of meaning, has been assumed. Some of the difficulties which occur when an attempt is made to make this distinction more exact have been alluded to in Chapter 4.

The sense in which a symbol, sign, word, or sentence "has meaning" is very difficult to specify; so difficult, in fact, that both linguists and lexicographers try to avoid talking about meaning at all. The former substitute for "meaning" the concept of a "significant sequence of morphemes," and the latter, the concept of synonymy. With reference to synonymy, Quine points out that:

What happens in this maneuver is that we fix on one important context of the baffling word "meaning," namely the context *"alike in* meaning," and resolve to treat this whole context in the spirit of a single word "synonymous," thus not being tempted to seek meanings as intermediary entities. But, even supposing that the notion of synonymy can eventually be provided with a satisfactory criterion, still this maneuver only takes care of the one context of the word "meaning"—the context "alike in meaning." Does the word also have other contexts that should concern linguists? Yes, there is certainly one more—the context "having meaning." [1]

Whether or not there can be significant discussion of "alike in meaning," even though "having meaning" remains undefined, is a matter which, for the moment, can be put aside. But a consideration of what happens when the concept of meaning is eliminated in favor of the concept of "significant sequence" will help to bring into focus the concept of meaning as a continuum.

Quine notes that the class of significant sequences must include not only all such sequences which have been uttered or written down but also all such sequences that *could* be uttered. We are led, he says, to the use of the contrary-to-fact conditional to define the membership of the class of significant sentences. Another name for the contrary-to-fact conditional is the "possible," as contrasted with the actual.

Whitehead is our source for the insight that one of the properties which distinguishes the actual from the possible is that whereas the actual is finite and atomic, the possible is a continuum. Here is the first suggestion that the hitherto intractable problem of meaning may be illuminated, if not solved, by recognizing that since meaning involves the possible, it may have the properties of a continuum, *i.e.*, the class of sentences that could be uttered may reasonably be considered to be a nondenumerable infinite class.

We may approach this problem from another direction by considering briefly, from an historical view, some of the difficulties which have attended discussions of meaning.

In this historical resume many necessary qualifications have been sacrificed in the cause of brevity. No footnotes and specific references to texts have been included because the purpose of this resume is not to establish a doctrine or to decide among competing doctrines, but to illustrate the historical tradition underlying modern discussions of meaning and to suggest an alternative to these doctrines.

The dialogues of Plato were concerned in large part with

Meaning as a Continuum

exploring the "meaning" of certain concepts, ranging from simple notions, such as "chair," "table," "food," to ethical notions like "justice," "goodness," "beauty," and mathematical notions like "triangularity," "straight," "point," etc. Plato was concerned with the problem of discerning and describing a permanent structure of meaning underlying the changing flux of human experience, with what John Dewey has called *The Quest for Certainty*. Plato asserted that beyond the changing arbitrary use of language could be discerned an eternal realm of "ideas" or meanings. These meanings, which were dimly apprehended in sense experience, could be discerned by a dialectical process of pure reason, which was essentially a gradual turning away from the flux of experience to a contemplation of the eternal essences and meanings.

Aristotle argued against this separation of sense and reason (as did Plato himself in some of his later dialogues), and held that "ideas" were inherent in things. He pointed out that if a chair and the idea of a chair were two things there would have to be a relation between them and hence an idea of this relation. This, in turn, would generate a relation between the relations and the idea of the relation, *ad infinitum*. This is known in the history of philosophy as "the third term argument." It was regarded as a strong argument because the ancient world found unpalatable an infinite realm of ideas or essences. What Aristotle dimly saw and rejected was a dense nondenumerable infinite, *i.e.*, a continuum.

Whitehead has remarked that European philosophy can be looked upon as a series of footnotes to Plato. One of the major facts justifying this remark is the controversy over universals which dominated medieval philosophy and theology. With reference to the relation of particulars to universals (of words to meanings) there were three views which are known as realism, conceptualism, and nominalism. Realism was essentially a restatement of the Platonic position. The universe consisted not only of particular things but of universals or essences. Thus blue is to be considered not only as a characteristic of this or that object but as an independently existing universal "blueness"; and particular entities are blue because they exhibit the character of "blueness." "Blueness" differs from this or that blue thing in being eternal and unchanging, *i.e.*, a universal. Hence, the meaning of the term "blue" considered by itself and divorced from any context is just the universal "blueness." The importance of this notion in the analysis of meaning is that it provides a realm of objective meanings which differ both from words and physical events.

Meaning Relation

Blue (word)   Blue book (physical object)   Blueness (universal)

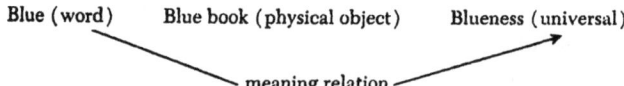

meaning relation

It might be thought that the universals could be dispensed with and that the meaning of "blue" could reside in a physical entity to which the term referred. But since the blue in book is not the same physical color as the blue of a teacup, it follows that the meaning of the term "blue" changes as its reference to different physical objects changes. Gottlob Frege has pointed out that meaning must be distinguished from reference. The two phrases, "the evening star" and "the morning star" have the same reference but not the same meaning. Further, many terms and phrases have meaning, even though they have no reference to physical entities, *e.g.*, the present King of France, $\sqrt{-2}$, Pegasus will fly no more, etc. To avoid these results, and at the same time to avoid the doctrine of realism, the doctrine of conceptualism was elaborated.

Meaning as a Continuum 103

Conceptualism holds that universals do not exist independently but as concepts in the mind. The concepts "blueness," "triangularity," "justice," which are the meanings of the terms "blue," "triangle," and "just" are thus creations of the mind; they are concepts which the mind has made by a process of abstraction from the physical entities or events which exhibit these characteristics. Hence the meaning relation becomes a relation between words and concepts and can be pictured:

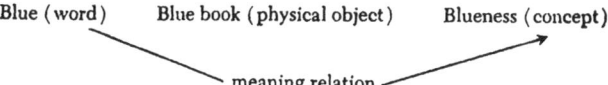

Blue (word)   Blue book (physical object)   Blueness (concept)
                    meaning relation

Conceptualism must, however, answer the criticism that it leads to subjectivism and the destruction of objective meanings and objective truth. If my meaning of "blue" consists of just the concept I have abstracted from my own set of experiences, and your meaning of "blue" is just the concept which you have abstracted from your set of experiences, what warrant is there for assuming an identity of meaning between my use of the term and your use of the term? This subjectivity or difference in meaning was not considered a serious matter for such concepts as "blue," or "hot," or "cold," etc.; but differences in the meaning of triangle could not be tolerated by mathematics and differences in the meaning of goodness, faith, charity, etc. could not be tolerated by the church. Conceptualism could only be saved from being heretical if it found a basis for universal meaning. It found such a basis by universalizing the process of abstraction, that is, it viewed abstraction not as a natural activity which differed from mind to mind but as a rational activity alike in all minds. This rational activity with which God has endowed man provides the insurance that a concept in A's mind is identical with a concept in B's mind. The relation of term to concept is thus universalized and science and religion are saved.

Another doctrine, nominalism, was part of a general attack on reason by those theologians of the Middle Ages who wished to emphasize the primacy of faith and mysticism at the expense of reason. The nominalist not only denied the existence of universals, but attempted to reduce concepts to names or terms whose meanings were completely exhausted by reference to particular objects. "Blue" became a word which referred to this or that blue object; and "goodness" became a word which referred to this or that good act. The mind used these words as signs, but it was not necessary, said the nominalists, to hypostatize a system of concepts as carriers of meaning or as mediators between words and things. A word could refer to a number of things by being a nonspecific sign; that is, become a general term referring to a collection of particular things. Such a use of signs did not require any perception of a "common characteristic" nor the development by the mind of a general concept.

Such a view leads to a complete relativism of meanings, not only among individuals, but in an individual's own use of a term. This bothered the nominalists not one whit, any more than it disturbed the sophists against whom Plato argued, since it broke down the pretensions of reason to discover truth and left the field to faith and revelation. As for imaginary numbers, false propositions, or propositions about imaginary objects, their meaning was accounted for by referring them to particular ideas in the mind.

In the modern period, except for the continuing tradition of Thomism, realism as a doctrine almost disappeared until it was revived by Charles S. Peirce in this country in the middle of the nineteenth century, and by G. E. Moore and Russell in England around the turn of the present century. But the controversy between conceptualism and nominalism was replayed between Locke and Berkeley. Locke advanced a doctrine of abstract or general ideas created by the mind from direct ideas of sensation and reflection. He used the notion of abstract ideas or concepts to explain not only how the mind which started as a *tabula rasa* developed ideas of classes or properties on the basis of particular sensations; but also how it could arrive at such ideas as "substance," "mind," and "God."

Berkeley took the extreme nominalist position for the same reason as his medieval predecessors. He wished to discredit the senses as a source of abstract knowledge and to eliminate the growing materialism of eighteenth-century science. Hence, he argued that the mind has no power to frame general ideas on the basis of sense experience. We can use "blue" as a word or a sign but we cannot conceive of a "blueness" which is not a particular blue having a particular shape; nor can we conceive of "heat" which is not a particular experience of a certain intensity; nor a shape that is not colored, etc. As for the ideas of substance or matter, these to Berkeley were just general signs which had no specific meaning or reference.

In recent times a number of additional doctrines of meaning have been adumbrated. Modern doctrines of behaviorism and pragmatism have tried to account for meaning as a reaction of a hearer to a statement, with the provision that the speaker may also be the hearer. In other words, the meaning of a sentence is in its behavioral effect. This doctrine has the peculiar consequence that a sentence is not true, false, or meaningful but will become meaningful, true, or false at some future time. However, to the extent that the reference to the future is also a reference to the possible, there is here a dim prevision of meaning as a continuum which is cut or particularized by particular sentences.

Russell and many logicians who followed him made meaning the property of statements, rather than terms, and ascribed to terms only incomplete meanings which were completed by their roles in statements. It should have been recognized that the meaning of any statement may be incomplete (determinable by its context) in just the same sense in which the meaning of a term is said to be incomplete. Here again there emerge properties of meaning which suggest a continuum.

A modern doctrine advanced by Tarski and the group of extreme formalists who follow him is retrogressive in its concept of a static meaning relation between statements and facts. This doctrine hopes to avoid the pitfalls which have been encountered by similar doctrines by first admitting that meaning and other semantic concepts cannot be formalized with reference to natural languages and secondly, by constructing a hierarchy of formal metalanguages, each one of which can contain formal definitions of the semantics of the one beneath it. This hierarchy presumably avoids Goedel's demonstration of the limits of formalization within any system or language:

It is possible to construct in the metalanguage methodologically correct and materially adequate definitions of the semantical concepts if and only if the metalanguage is equipped with variables of higher logical type than all the variables of the language which is the subject of investigation.[2]

Since our concern is with the meaning of natural languages and natural signs, Tarski's whole contribution becomes ir-

Meaning as a Continuum

relevant. Nevertheless, it seems important to illustrate the static and limited nature of the views advanced by Tarski and his followers.

The basis of Tarski's position is the very important distinction between languages *in* which we talk about nonlinguistic facts and languages *about* which we talk. When we talk about a language we can indicate this fact by using quotation marks. Consider the sentences

(1) New York is the largest city in the United States.
(2) "New York" is the name of the capital of New York.
(3) New York has seven letters.
(4) "New York" has seven letters.

(1) is a sentence about a city. (2) is a sentence about a name. (3) is false. (4) is true. This distinction permits the following definition of truth and presumably similar definitions can be used for other semantic concepts.

(5) "It is snowing" is true if and only if it is snowing.

There is a daring and deceiving simplicity about this doctrine. In the first place, Tarski admits that it is only relevant to what he calls the classical theory of truth which holds that the truth of a sentence resides in its correspondence with the facts. As a matter of fact, no scientific system is true in this sense. The coherence and operational theories of truth, whatever their difficulties, certainly present a more adequate concept of scientific truth than the correspondence theory. Secondly, the example used by Tarski, which seems to link a simple sentence with a simple physical fact, tends to be accepted by inspection. But suppose for his example there is substituted:

(6) "God exists" is true if and only if God exists.

There is no separate, discrete fact or state of affairs which can be compared with the sentence "God exists" to establish a relation of formal equivalence between the sentence and the fact.

If Tarski should reply that the formal equivalence doesn't hold between sentence and fact, but between a sentence in one language and a sentence in another, this can be granted; but then it becomes difficult to see why the equivalence of sentences in the same language is a purely formal fact without semantic significance, whereas the equivalence of a sentence in one language with a sentence in another language is presumed to have such content. Either Tarski's conclusion is purely formal, *i.e.*, true by definition, in which case it has no semantic content, or it must appeal to an experiential relation between any language and a set of facts, in which case there is a genuine semantic content but a content which is outside any formal system even if it should involve an infinite hierarchy of metalanguages.

As has been noted, this encapsulated history of doctrines of meaning does violence to the subtleties and qualifications with which a great number of brilliant thinkers developed their views. But it does serve to indicate that the problem of meaning has a long and thorny history and is not apt to yield to any simple solution such as that offered by neophytes in this field who presume that the problem of meaning is a new problem, contemporary with the problem of mechanical translation.

In discussing the word "meaning" Quine noted that it has at least two contexts, namely, "alike in meaning" and "having meaning." Quine's use of the term "context" is itself a curious solecism. Obviously, he wished to avoid talking about "the meaning of alike in meaning" or "the meaning of having meaning"; but why "context"? In ordinary usage, rather than

Meaning as a Continuum 109

"context," one might expect that "alike in meaning" would be considered a relation between two terms or sentences (pMq) and that "having a meaning" would be considered a property of a term or sentence (Ma).

The difficulty with this view is that it creates the problem of explaining what kind of relation "M" is. It seems clear that it is not a physical relation like "bigger than," "father of," or "cause of," and it is not a formal logical relation like "and," "or," and "not." It might, of course, be a mental relation, but since the whole point of contemporary logical and linguistic analysis, as exemplified in the work of linguists such as Harris and logicians such as Carnap and Tarski, is to get rid of mental relations in favor of physical and formal relations, a mental relation of meaning would be anathema. Similarly, with the predicate function (Ma). What kind of property is "meaning"? It is obviously not a physical property in the sense that "red," "heavy," or "long" are physical properties; and it is not a logical property such as being "well-formed" or tautological. And it cannot be a "mental" property because, as has been said, such properties are not allowed in formal analysis.

The expression "context" may avoid these questions temporarily by indicating that questions of meaning are resolvable by examining other words (contexts) in which the word "meaning" appears. I think this is not the case, and it is not suggested that Quine holds this view. I think Quine used this expression to avoid getting mired down in questions he did not wish to discuss in this particular paper "The Problem of Meaning in Linguistics," because it is relatively simple to show that context does not mean physical context, namely, the shapes to the right or left of a word, nor the sounds before and after it, but the context of meaning. To explain meaning by referring to contexts is like explaining the perception of red by noting that it is a perception of a color.

If we accept, then, for the moment, the systematic ambiguity of the two contexts "alike in meaning" and "having meaning," we should like at this time to suggest a third context, namely, "being a meaning." In logical terms this means that meaning is neither a relation nor a property, but an individual or a variable.

The context "being a meaning" has an important heuristic value; it serves to restore a distinction which has tended to be quietly, although not decently, buried by modern formalists (like an insane cousin put away in an institution whom none of the family talks about). A sentence or a statement may be said without bizarreness of idiom to "have meaning" or to be "alike in meaning" to other sentences; but it would be bizarre to say of a sentence that it "*is* a meaning." On the other hand, although it is accepted to speak of propositions as "having meaning" or as being "alike in meaning," it is also acceptable to say of propositions (as distinguished from sentences) that they *are* meanings.

The substitution of the term "sentence" or "statement" for the term "proposition" in logical discourse is again a contribution of modern formalists, beginning with Wittgenstein and Carnap and reaching its apotheosis in Tarski. *Principia Mathematica* uses the terms "propositions," "propositional calculus," and "propositional functions." The terms "sentence" and "sentential function" do not appear in its table of contents, although in Russell's introduction to Volume 1 the term "statement" is used occasionally instead of the term "proposition"; but this usage only occurs in nonformal discussions. All the formal discussions concern propositions and not statements nor sentences. Wittgenstein used the term "atomic sentence" rather than "atomic proposition"; and in Carnap's work, the expressions "sentential calculus" and "sentence" replace the expressions "proposition" and "propositional calculus" almost completely. Quine, in his *Mathematical Logic,* discusses statements. The words "proposition" and "propositional function" appear in its index only as references to the words "statement" and "statement matrix." The index to Quine's *Methods of Logic* no longer contains the word "proposition"; and "propositional function" appears merely as a reference to notes explaining earlier usages of the term. Church, on the other hand, reintroduces the use of the term "propositional calculus" as a name of a type of logistic system, but the elements of such a calculus are symbols and formulae, rather than terms and propositions. In his *New Foundations* Quine also uses "formula" instead of either "proposition" or "statement." Tarski, as has been indicated, carries this development to its limits. He seems not to realize that there might be a difference between a sentence and a proposition. He is concerned exclusively with the sentential calculus and truth as properties of sentences in formalized languages. However, he does recognize a problem in this connection, to which he bows in passing.

Statements (sentences) are always treated here as a particular kind of expression, and thus as linguistic entities. Nevertheless, when the terms "expression," "statement," etc., are interpreted as names of concrete series of printed signs, various formulations which occur in this work do not appear to be quite correct, and give the appearance of a widespread error which consists in identifying expressions of like shape. . . . In order to avoid . . . the introduction of superfluous complications into the discussion, which would be connected among other things with the necessity of using the concept of likeness of shape, it is convenient to stipulate that terms like "word," "expression," "sentence," etc., do not denote concrete series of signs but whole classes of such series which are of like shape with the series given; only in this sense shall we regard quotation-mark names as individual names of expressions.[3]

The problem which Tarski faces here is unavoidable. If sentences are physical facts, then no sentence is ever repeatable. For that matter, no symbol is ever repeatable. Tarski's suggested solution, which is to regard a sentence as a whole class of a series of marks which are of like shape, is really no solution because the notion of being of like shape is not formal. To say of a mark on one page that it is the same symbol as a mark on another page is to say that there is more to being a symbol than merely to be a mark of a certain shape. What this means is that any formal development, however rigorous and however prolonged, is only an interlude between an informal beginning and an informal end. Whitehead, in the preface to *Process and Reality*, states that among other prevalent habits of thought it is necessary to repudiate "the trust in language as an adequate expression of propositions" and he asserts categorically in the first chapter "that no verbal statement is the adequate expression of a proposition."

The neglect of this view by modern formalists and the way in which most of them play fast and loose with the distinction between sentences and propositions is a major aberration of modern science. It should not be forgotten that as a creative mathematician and logician, Whitehead is one of the greatest figures of all time. What makes him great is that he combined technical virtuosity with profound insight. He was followed to a considerable extent by young virtuosos who thought it sufficient to concentrate on technique, *i.e.*,

Meaning as a Continuum 113

the manipulation of symbols. Here is an instance which illustrates the important public service which could be performed by critics of science. If a musician had technical skill alone, without depth of expression and insight, the musical critics would say so and dismiss him as a journeyman at best and a clod at worst. There are similar journeymen and clods in the fields of logic and mathematics. But because there are almost no critics who understand the technical manipulations with which they busy themselves, they succeed in their protestations that "technique is all"; that the manipulation of symbols is an end in itself; and that propositions and meanings can be either neglected or even ruled out as nonexistent. There is no intention here to belittle technique; without it a musician or mathematician, however deep and profound his insight, remains mute.

What, then, are propositions which language seeks to express? They are, according to Whitehead, impure prehensions, which play a role in the coming to be of an actual entity or an occasion. Every actual entity has a physical datum, the physical occasions in its past. In addition, every actual entity will establish the relevance of some selection from the eternal objects (essences) considered as pure possibilities which may be realized or dismissed into irrelevance by the process of coming to be of the actual entity. Certain high-grade actual entities will also experience propositions which are theories about the relevance of certain possibilities to a definite nexus of actual entities. The actual entity entertaining the proposition entertains the notion of the possible characterization of the actual entities in its own past. Thus it can be said that propositions function in experience as mediators between the brute fact of the past and the pure possibility of the future. They express the graded relevance of some possibilities for some actual entities. The prehension of this relevance is experiential, that is to say, *actual*, rather than *verbal*. Any sentence merely attempts to describe a proposition which is a real fact in the experience of an actual entity. This doctrine does not make propositions "mental," any more than physics is mental because it is an empirical science having its basis in experience.

This brief summary of a very profound and subtle doctrine is not apt to win conviction, especially from those to whom words like "prehension," "feeling," "actual entity," etc., are strange and unfamiliar. There is perhaps another way to disclose the nature of propositions in a manner which brings home the distinction between "having a meaning" and "being a meaning." It is well recognized, even by those entirely unsympathetic with his views, that Whitehead replaces the concept of "thing" with the concept of "process" in very much the same sense in which the billiard ball atoms of the nineteenth century have been replaced in physics by patterns of energy. In ordinary language a "thing" has properties, *e.g.*, we say "this table is red" and if propositions are things, they might be expected to have properties, *e.g.*, meaning, truth, falsity. Sentences are things and sentences have properties, *e.g.*, they are well-formed, two inches long, written in ink, and express propositions. Propositions, however, are not things; they are elements of process. To bring this point home, Whitehead uses the expression "propositional feelings." Another way of saying this is that meaning with reference to propositions is neither a relation nor a property, but an individual. A proposition *is* a meaning and to be a meaning is to be an element or cut in the process of experience.

By this time the reason for the seeming mystery and intractability of meaning ought to be clear. A sentence is related

Meaning as a Continuum

to a proposition as a more or less adequate expression of the meaning, which the proposition is. Hence, the relation of a sentence to a proposition can be called a meaning relationship. Sentences also, as symbols, have the property of being expressions of propositions and, as such, have the property of meaning derivatively. Philology and grammar, as normative disciplines, tell us how to express meanings more adequately; linguistics, as a descriptive science, describes the sounds and shapes with which we attempt to express meaning. But a proposition is just the meaning that it is; it is an element of a continuum of meaning.

So far it has been shown that in various solutions of the problem of meaning there has been a vague, though persistent, recognition that in some sense meanings are not discrete and separable entities in the sense that words are. A written word is nicely marked off from other words by spaces at both ends. Sentences are marked off from other sentences by capitals and periods. Similarly, sounded words or morphemes are marked off from one another by periods of silence. It is pretty obvious that as contrasted with words and sentences, meanings are not marked off from one another by little spaces and times. It may even be suggested that there are not many meanings, but one meaning like one space, which is divisible but not divided. Propositions may particularize, *i.e.*, make cuts in meaning space, in just the same way a body marks out a cut in space without destroying the continuity of space. However suggestive this analogy, it remains vague: before it can be said that a doctrine of meaning as a continuum can be offered as a substitute for any or all of the traditional doctrines, this vague analogy must be replaced by a specific description of a continuum and a reasoned argument for assigning such a description to the realm of meaning.

116   Meaning as a Continuum

We have looked for a description of continua which could be applicable to meaning in Huntington's classical monograph, *The Continuum and Other Types of Serial Order*. In this monograph, Huntington first defines a series and then defines a continuum as a certain type of dense, nondenumerable series. What is required for meaning is a notion of a nonordered continuum, that is, of a dense, nondenumerable class. N-dimensional series in Huntington's sense would be included in the class meaning; but it is not likely that the totality of meaning has serial order. There seems no reason why the definition of such a class could not be formulated in fairly exact terms, although such a definition will not be undertaken here. There is a prior requirement to make clear in more concrete intuitive terms why meaning is a continuum.

In the first place, the conjunction or sum of propositions is a proposition in just the same sense that the sum of numbers is a number and the sum of spaces is a space. There is no "longest proposition," any more than there is a "largest number." This establishes the infinity of meaning but not its density and nondenumerability. The set of real numbers which is dense and nondenumerable can represent a similar set of propositions, namely, the totality of the propositions which assert the existence of each real number.

Finally, any meaning, which as a proposition is the characterization of a nexus of actual entities by a selected set of eternal objects, has relevance to a nondenumerable set of possibilities which constitute a nondenumerable penumbra of meanings clustering around any given meaning. The graded relevance of nonrealized possibilities to any actual proposition is what gives propositions different meanings to different people. The simple proposition, "this stone is grey," is not only the positive prehension of the characterization of a nexus of actual entities by a particular character selected from all those possible; but the very meaning of the proposition is infused with the negative prehensions of what the stone is not. Everyone recognizes the sense in which the extent of the penumbra of relevant meanings contributes to aesthetic experience, but one is apt to neglect backgrounds when one is concerned with the truth or falsity of particular propositions.

In the last analysis, experience is primarily aesthetic, an affair of feeling and not logic. Logicians abstract from the matrix of experience and consider only certain formal relations of propositions and the sentences which express them. But—and here we end on the same note with which we began—to take as the sole reality the result of an abstraction from a concrete process, is the basic error of formalism and one of the most widespread modern scientific aberrations.

ADDENDUM: ON SCIENTIFIC
ABERRATIONS

The original plan and impetus of this book were derived in large measure from a book which appeared in 1934, bearing the innocuous title, *An Enquiry into the Nature of Certain Nineteenth Century Pamphlets*, by John Carter and Graham Pollard. The Carter and Pollard *Enquiry* is an account of a bibliographical investigation into a wholesale literary forgery, the exposition of which shook the learned world of two continents. The authors, whose suspicions had been aroused by discrepancies in the literary history of a reputed privately printed edition of Elizabeth Barrett Browning's *Sonnets from the Portuguese,* ultimately uncovered one of the largest and most successful literary forging operations of all time. The forger had been successful not only in placing copies of his work in most of the major literary collections in this country and in England, but he had involved a great many distinguished critics and book collectors in his operations. He followed a simple routine of presenting copies of his forgeries to critics known to have an interest in the authors and to such libraries as the British Museum. Only after the delighted critics and libraries had noted and written about the valuable works which had come into their possession did the forger "find" other copies, which he then proceeded to sell to rich

British and American collectors, basing the books' authenticity on statements issued by the British Museum and other unimpeachable critics. The forger was honored for his services to British literature and his collection and its great catalog were purchased by the British Museum. It can be seen that exposing such a web would be resented not only by the spider, but by all the distinguished institutions and literary figures who had been caught in it.

Actually, it was the very wholesale nature of his operations which protected the forger. One might question the authenticity of a particular volume, but how does one dare to question an activity which seems to involve a major portion of bibliography and book collecting in England and the United States? The authors express the problem which this presented:

> If we ourselves are beyond being surprised at the results of our investigation, we are fully alive to the fact that their unexpected nature is likely to induce not merely shock but incredulity in the minds of some of our readers. A man who has always accepted a certain book is nevertheless prepared (even against his inclination, if he owns a copy) to believe it spurious, provided that the proof seems to him satisfactory. But if it is not a question of a single book, but thirty or forty, what then? We are perfectly confident that in every case where proof is claimed, that proof *is* satisfactory: but the very magnitude of the numbers involved is bound to provoke some scepticism in anyone unprepared for such a wholesale exposure of clay feet among the accepted idols. The sceptic will then very properly ask: "When was this fraud perpetrated? and by whom? How did these books achieve their position? and why have they remained unchallenged so long?" [1]

In this book certain scientific activities and claims have been investigated. If this investigation had been concerned with the activities of a single individual or institution only, it would have presented a much simpler problem; but one considers and comments on the validity of activities supported or carried on by such institutions as the Rockefeller Foundation, Massachusetts Institute of Technology, Harvard University, the RAND Corporation, Ramo-Wooldridge, etc., at one's peril. It might be presumed that any scientific activity engaged in by such organizations is *ipso facto* immune from criticism by virtue of the nature of the agencies. This, of course, is exactly the situation faced by Messrs. Carter and Pollard. Nevertheless, they followed where their investigation led them and were not deterred by the fact that it led them to question the sacredness of sacred cows.

One of the things that Carter and Pollard discovered was that whole structures of literary comment were based upon a single sentence, repeated and elaborated upon by many different people. What looked to be a great mass of evidence for the authenticity of the forgeries was all traceable to A quoting B, who had quoted C, who had quoted D, who had quoted E, etc. Similarly, it has been shown that with reference to scientific activities examined in this study, what looks to be a great mass of serious, detailed work carried out by scientists of distinguished reputation evaporates when examined without prejudice. There are in the literature on mechanical translation, learning-machines, automata, etc., a great many names of nonexistent machines whose operations are described and debated as though they were real. The whole performance takes on the character of the behavior of the tailors in "The Emperor's New Clothes."

It should be made clear here that the parallelism between this investigation and that conducted by Carter and Pollard does not extend to the question of fraud. There is no implication here that the scientific claims which have been examined were advanced as a deliberate fraud, but only that they represent aberrations as unwarranted and unreal as the literary provenience of the pamphlets discussed by Carter and Pollard. On the other hand, regardless of the intentions of those involved in these aberrations, the public which accepts the scientist as the high priest of the twentieth century is betrayed.

The criticism of science in the twentieth century is a kind of *lèse majesté* somewhat equivalent to criticizing the Roman Catholic Church in the twelfth century. It is seldom realized that every form of intellectual endeavor with the exception of science has both practitioners and informed critics. These critics in the fields of poetry, fiction, drama, painting, sculpture, music, etc., not only function as interpreters of the practitioners to the general public, but as critics who compare and evaluate the work of the practitioners. A critic who never wrote a poem, composed a score, or painted a picture may perform the valuable service of noting that a particular poem, score, or painting is uninspired, shoddy, or imitative. Furthermore, no one seriously supposes that the work of such critics constitutes censorship or restriction on the free creative spirits of poets, musicians, or painters. But scientists have insisted that any criticism of their work does constitute censorship or a failure to appreciate the necessity for "basic" (which sometimes should be read as trivial or useless) research. Scientists have even asserted their immunity from any accountability for the public funds they expend, as will be recollected by remembering the first National Science Foundation Bill which former President Truman was courageous enough to veto.

In all of the public discussion about the missile gap between ourselves and the Russians, every group other than our scientists has been blamed at one time or other. The cause of our failures, it is said, is the blindness of the Administration, the jealousy of the armed services, the political maneuvering of Congress, the venality of our corporations, or the apathy of the general public. No scientist or nonscientist has said what seems clearly to be the case, namely, *that our scientists may not be good enough* and that in this area, at least, the Russian scientists are better educated and/or smarter.

One of the reasons for this ostrich-like attitude is that the term "scientist" or "science" has taken on evaluative overtones and now means good scientist and important science. A "bad" scientist in the movies is depicted as someone who is cruel to his mother or in the pay of the communists, whereas in fact, a bad scientist, like a bad poet or a bad musician, is someone whose work is bad. There is bad science in just the same sense as there is bad poetry or bad music. There are thousands of scientists who are in science in just the same sense that other people are in religion, in politics, in music, in advertising, or in retailing. They are ordinary men with an ordinary percentage of devoted men and self-seekers; wise men and fools; honest men and knaves. Scientists today will admit that there were stupid scientists and scientists who made bad mistakes, but they will usually make such judgments only about the past. The errors of science are presumably only those which occurred long ago, and the public stereotype of a scientist is an image of a brilliant man who couldn't make a mistake or throw away millions of dollars of other people's money because he is too stupid or vain to face the fact of his own incompetence.

This book has not been concerned with the evaluation of the work of individual scientists *per se,* but with present day aberrations of the scientific enterprise in general. It would be readily admitted by scientists that there were scientific aberrations in the past, namely, such enterprises as the science of alchemy or the science of phrenology. And it would be admitted that on the fringes of respectable scientific activity there are pseudo sciences like astrology, dianetics, spiritualism, and numerology. But is the line between cloth and fringe so sharp? What about telepathy, parapsychology, and general semantics? And beyond these, what about psychoanalysis, the science of progressive education, or the science of public opinion polls, not to mention the science of hotel keeping and cosmetology? These questions are designed to indicate that neither public acceptance nor academic respectability is any guarantee of the soundness and legitimacy of a scientific enterprise.

There does exist a considerable literature of debate on whether or not this or that area of human endeavor should be called a science. In the field of psychology different schools, *e.g.*, association psychologists, experimental psychologists, introspectionists, behaviorists, or psychoanalysts, have at different times insisted on the scientific character of their work and have rejected the claims of other schools to be called scientific. There has been congressional debate concerning the right of the social sciences to be called sciences and thus find a niche within the activities of the National Science Foundation. Those who practice the science of advertising, based on the science of sampling and the science of calculating and modifying motivations, have learned that the mantle of science will sell cigarettes, cosmetics, and breakfast foods. The problem here is that the word science has become an accolade, a laurel with which an enterprise is crowned and made good.

There was a time when the word religion carried a similar

evaluational content. To be religious was *ipso facto* good; to be nonreligious or irreligious was *ipso facto* bad. But then the word lost this evaluational content and it became proper to talk about the religion of communism, meaning thereby a faith in or an adherence to communism. Since most of us think such adherence bad, it is now acceptable to talk of good or bad religion. In other words, it is generally recognized that the important fact about religion is not that someone believes, but *what* someone believes in.

A similar metamorphosis of the term "science" would be a healthy change. Let anyone who wishes call himself a "scientist" and his activity a "science." Then we can stop quarreling about the meaning of a word and substitute for it the more important task of examining the value of the activity itself. The way things are now, if someone can get by with preempting the use of the term "science" he is relatively free from exposure as a charlatan even if he is one. Even in the extreme case of astronomy and astrology, if astrologers claimed to be as scientific as astronomers, I would give them *carte blanche* to the use of the word. For this *carte blanche* would immediately rob the word of its magical properties. If being a scientist were no more remarkable than being tall or short, fat or thin, the word "science" could not be used to peddle nostrums to a gullible public. An activity carried out by any public or private body would then be evaluated as an activity, and its sponsors could not hide from scrutiny or frighten off investigators by insisting on the pure scientific nature of their intentions.

The relation between the science of astronomy and the science of astrology offers certain intriguing possibilities for speculation. Let us suppose that a university had a good telescope but only a small operating budget in its astronomy

Addendum 125

department and thus could not make full use of its physical facilities. Suppose further that to a meeting of the astronomy faculty an ambitious assistant professor presents a scheme to raise funds for the department by selling time and service to astrologers. The head of the department might be horrified and refuse to pander even on his spare time, that is, on the unused time of the telescope, to an activity so unscientific and so manifestly false.

At this point the young professor, who knows that thousands of honest newspapers carry daily horoscopes, may say to his chief: "It is logically possible that the movement of planets through the zodiac has an influence on human conduct or action. There is nothing contradictory in such a possibility." The department head would have to admit this fact, but if he were an honest man, he would tell the assistant to go to blazes. As for the assistant, if he really disbelieved in the possibility of zodiacal influences and yet used his skills to peddle astrological information, he would be a fraud like the forger run to earth by Carter and Pollard. But if he really believed that pure logical possibility was all a scientist needed to justify a course of action, then he would be a fool and not a rogue.

Consider a similar case and one more directly related to the theme of this book. Suppose a university has acquired a large and expensive computer which is so efficient that it can do all the necessary computing for a day in a fraction of the available time. Seeing this large and expensive machine sitting idle, a young assistant professor suggests that it might be interesting to use the damned thing to translate languages or simulate brains or play chess. If his chief asks the young professor whether the machine can really do these things, the assistant may reply that there is nothing logically impossible about such machine activities. There is no fraud here unless the assistant knows or believes that in the end the machine won't be able to translate or act like a brain. But if he proceeds on the basis of the pure logical possibility of such activities, he is as asinine as the honest astrologer in the department of astronomy.

The aberrations with which we have been concerned are not such easy old targets as astrology or alchemy, but that new star in the scientific firmament, cybernetics. Cybernetics was described by its founder, Norbert Wiener, as the science of control in men and machines. It is one of the major contentions of cybernetics that massive analogies exist between control functions in men and machines so that the design of machine controls can constitute a contribution to neurophysiology, and the study of neurophysiology can contribute to both the understanding and design of machines. Undoubtedly analogies exist between men and machines and the study of such analogies is a valid intellectual enterprise. But as Von Neumann and others have pointed out, there is an enormous logical and practical difference between analogy and identity. There are profound differences between the operations of men and machines; and the conversion of the similarity relationship, which is the basis of analogy, to the formal logical relation of identity is a logical fallacy which has had in this instance very unfortunate consequences. In the history of science and philosophy this fallacy has led many times to the methodological fallacy of reductionism. For example, an explanation of heard sounds in terms of frequency and amplitude of vibrations has led by reduction to the false assertion that the heard sounds are identical with the amplitude and frequency of vibrations. In the area of cybernetics, the analogies between neurological networks

Addendum 127

and the electrical networks of computers have led by reduction to the false assertion that neurological networks are identical with the electrical circuits in computers.

There is no need to expand further on this point. It is important, however, to note that Von Neumann, who was perhaps the most profound student of this generation of the analogy between men and machines, predicted before his death that there was more to be learned about machines from the study of neurology than could be learned about neurology from the study of machines.

Because of a tendency to confuse words as sounds or written symbols with meaning, a topic with which several of the previous chapters have been concerned, what has been said so far about the use and abuse of the words "science" and "scientists" may be taken by some to represent an attack on "eggheads," on learning, and on methods of rational inquiry. In order to lay this ghost once and for all, let it be stated now, without any equivocation, that this book is soundly based on the maxim that "Ye shall know the truth, and the truth shall make you free"; and on an abiding faith that the process of rational inquiry and the increase and diffusion of knowledge are the noblest ends of man. It is because of these views that it is necessary to point out the degree of corruption which has invested the terms "science" and "scientists." It may be that these words can someday be rehabilitated and restored to their former stature, but this prospect is dubious. It might require, for example, stringent laws against the abuse of these words by advertisers, which seems an unlikely eventuality. There have been similar cases of corruption of words. In 1940 Archibald MacLeish, in his epoch-making article, "The Irresponsibles," wrote sorrowfully about the corruption of such terms as "freedom," "democracy," and "patriotism." The National Socialist movement in Germany corrupted once and for all the term "socialism" as the name for a major ideal of the nineteenth century. When a term becomes corrupted in this fashion, it creates a burden of examining the many and perhaps contradictory ways in which it is used. It is not enough to accept the fact that someone calls himself a scientist or calls his activity a science. It is necessary to go further and ask what the man knows and exactly what he is doing. No law can take away from an astrologer the right to refer to his work as the science of astrology. On the other hand, it can be said that the science of astrology is an activity generally followed by rogues and dupes, with perhaps a sprinkling of sentimental antiquarians. Similarly, those who assert the identity of men and machines, who promise us on scientific grounds that within ten years computers will discover important mathematical theorems, write worthwhile music, take over the major part of the field of psychology, and dethrone the current world chess champion, are latter-day soothsayers.

All noble things, says Spinoza, are as difficult as they are rare. So it is with respect to science and scientific advance in the computer and data processing field. Genuine advances are difficult and rare. And even more rarely are they the product of prophecy and the premature announcement of what someone expects to do but has not done.

REFERENCES

1: *INTRODUCTION*
 1. W. V. O. Quine, *Mathematical Logic* (Cambridge, Harvard University Press), 1951, p. 318.
 2. Ibid., p. 321.

2: *POSSIBILITY AS A GUIDE*
 1. A. M. Turing, "Can a Machine Think?" in *The World of Mathematics*, ed. by James R. Newman (New York, Simon and Schuster, Inc., 1956), vol. 4, p. 2109.
 2. Ernest Nagel and James R. Newman, "Goedel's Proof," in *The World of Mathematics*, vol. 3, p. 1695.
 3. A. M. Turing, "Can a Machine Think?" p. 2107.
 4. Russell Maloney, "Inflexible Logic," in *The World of Mathematics, vol. 4,* pp. 2262–67.
 5. Ibid., p. 2263.
 6. Ibid., p. 2264.
 7. Ibid., p. 2265.
 8. Ibid., p. 2267.
 9. W. R. Ashby, "Design for an Intelligence-Amplifier," in *Automata Studies,* ed. by C. E. Shannon and J. McCarthy (Princeton, Princeton University Press, 1956), p. 217.
 10. Warren Weaver, "Translation," in *Machine Translation of Languages,* ed. by William N. Locke and A. Donald Booth (New York, John Wiley and Sons, Inc., 1955), p. 22.
 11. W. S. McCulloch and Walter Pitts, "A Logical Calculus of the Ideas Immanent in Nervous Activity," in *The Bulletin of Mathematical Biophysics,* ed. by N. Rashevsky (Colorado Springs, The Dentan Printing Co., 1943), vol. 5, pp. 115–33.

130   3: Mechanical Translation

12. *Information Theory, Third London Symposium,* ed. by Colin Cherry (London, Academic Press Inc., 1955), p. 230.

3: MECHANICAL TRANSLATION

1. W. S. McCulloch, "The Design of Machines to Simulate the Behavior of the Human Brain," in *IRE National Convention, 1955, Symposium,* p. 240.
2. A. G. Oettinger, ibid., p. 242.
3. George Crabbe (1754–1832), "The Library."
4. A. G. Oettinger, *Automatic Language Translation* (Cambridge, Harvard University Press, 1960), p. vii.
5. *Machine Translation of Languages,* ed. by William N. Locke and A. Donald Booth (New York, John Wiley and Sons, Inc., 1955).
6. A. G. Oettinger, *Automatic Language Translation,* p. 346.
7. *Machine Translation of Languages,* p. 1.
8. Yehoshua Bar-Hillel, *Current Research and Development in Scientific Documentation* (Washington, National Science Foundation, 1959), No. 5, p. 64.
9. *Machine Translation of Languages,* p. 24.
10. Ibid. p. 24.
11. S. C. Dodd, ibid., Chapter 10, pp. 165–73.
12. Erwin Reifler, ibid., p. 137.
13. Yehoshua Bar-Hillel, *Report on the State of Machine Translation in the United States and Great Britain* (Jerusalem, Hebrew University, 1959), p. 38.
14. Ibid., p. 39.
15. *Linguistic and Engineering Studies in the Automatic Translation of Scientific Russian into English* (Seattle, The University of Washington).
16. D. W. Moore, "The Design of a Practical Russian-English Mechanical Translator," *Engineering Analysis Appendix II,* ibid.
17. R. E. Wall Jr., "Some of the Economics of Machine Translation," *Engineering Analysis,* ibid.

4: LEARNING-MACHINES

1. A. M. Uttley, "Conditional Probability Machines and Con-

ditioned Reflexes," in *Automata Studies*, ed. by C. E. Shannon and J. McCarthy (Princeton University Press, 1956), p. 255.

2. Ibid., p. 257.

3. Norbert Wiener, *Cybernetics or Control and Communication in the Animal and the Machine* (New York, John Wiley and Sons, Inc., 1948), pp. 151–53.

4. A. Newell, J. C. Shaw, and H. A. Simon, "Chess-Playing Programs and the Problem of Complexity," in *IBM Journal of Research and Development* (1958), vol. 2, No. 4, p. 320.

5. Yehoshua Bar-Hillel, *Report on the State of Machine Translation in the United States and Great Britain* (Jerusalem, Hebrew University, 1959), p. 38.

5: *LINGUISTIC ANALYSIS*

1. Noam Chomsky, "Logical Structure in Language," in *American Documentation* (New York, Interscience Publishers, Inc., 1957), vol. VIII, No. 4, p. 284.

2. Ibid.

3. Ibid.

4. Noam Chomsky, "Three Models for the Description of Language," in *IRE Transactions on Information Theory*, vol. IT-2, No. 3, p. 113.

5. Noam Chomsky, *American Documentation*, vol. VIII, No. 4, p. 286.

6. Noam Chomsky, *IRE Transactions on Information Theory*, vol. IT-2, No. 3, p. 123.

7. Ibid., p. 114.

8. Ibid., p. 123.

9. Ibid., p. 123.

10. Noam Chomsky, *American Documentation*, vol. VIII, No. 4, p. 291.

11. Rudolf Carnap, *Meaning and Necessity, A Study in Semantics and Modal Logic* (Chicago, The University of Chicago Press, 1947), p. 5.

12. Z. S. Harris, "Linguistic Transformations for Information Retrieval," in *International Conference on Scientific Information, Area V, Preprints of Papers* (Washington, 1958), p. 129.

132   6: Man-Machine Relations

13. Ibid., p. 130.
14. Ibid., p. 128.
15. Yehoshua Bar-Hillel, *Report on the State of Machine Translation in the United States and Great Britain* (Jersualem, Hebrew University, 1959), p. 17.
16. *Current Research and Development in Scientific Documentation,* No. 5 (Washington, National Science Foundation, 1959).
17. Ibid., p. 23. (Itek Corporation).
18. Ibid., pp. 25–26. (Lockheed Aircraft Corporation).
19. Ibid., p. 30. (National Bureau of Standards).
20. Ibid., p. 36. (System Development Corporation).
21. Ibid., p. 38. (U. S. Patent Office).
22. Ibid., p. 43. (Western Reserve University).
23. Ibid., p. 46. (Zator Company).
24. Ibid., p. 51. (Arthur D. Little, Inc.).
25. Ibid., p. 52. (Cambridge Language Research Unit).
26. Ibid., p. 55. (Harvard University).
27. Ibid., p. 59. (Ramo-Wooldridge).
28. Ibid., p. 64. (Bar-Hillel, Hebrew University).

6: *MAN-MACHINE RELATIONS*

1. Douglas Aircraft Company, Inc. Engineering Department, El Segundo, California. Integrated Instrument Development Contract No. NONR 1076(00) Report No. ES-26040, September 13, 1955.
2. "It has become a popular sport in the past few years to describe brain functions in computing-machine terms and computing-machine functions in human behavioral terms and to get a good deal of satisfaction out of the notion that while it may take a year or two yet, we will certainly be able to understand mental function in computer terms before too long and will shortly thereafter be able to design really heavy-duty brains with greater speed and capacity, and increased reliability.

"While I am all in favor of such enthusiasms, on the basis that nothing succeeds like success, I believe I should risk the disapproval of some members of this group of investigators by pointing

6: Man-Machine Relations 133

out a type of circular reasoning which has been prevalent in their arguments. This is the fault of using a disguised form of an hypothesis to prove the hypothesis.

"To illustrate my point, I would like to tell you a true story about one of my colleagues whom I shall not name. This gentleman, a professor of considerable fame, was waiting to listen to a fight on the radio but because the fight was delayed in starting, he idly turned to the university station and heard a lecture already in progress with which he became very impressed, and to which he listened most attentively. Because he agreed so completely with the speaker's point of view, he availed himself of the invitation at the end of the lecture to send a postcard for a copy of the lecture. He was considerably taken aback when he received his copy to find a note attached asking whether he had lost the original copy as he himself had recorded the lecture on tape several months ago for later broadcast.

"By analogy with this story, I believe we have fallen into the trap of describing some brain functions in terms of present-day computer components and are then delighted to discover machine-like components in our description of brain function." O. H. Schmitt, "The Design of Machines to Simulate the Behavior of the Human Brain," in *IRE National Convention, 1955, Symposium*, p. 240–55.

3. A. G. Oettinger, ibid., pp. 241–42.
4. O. H. Schmitt, ibid., p. 251.
5. Marvin Minsky, ibid.
6. A. G. Oettinger, ibid., p. 242.
7. M. E. Maron, ibid., p. 249.
8. A. M. Turing, "Can a Machine Think?" in *The World of Mathematics*, ed. by James R. Newman (New York, Simon and Schuster, Inc., 1956), vol. 4, p. 2104.
9. Vittorio Somenzi, *Information Theory, Third London Symposium*, ed. by Colin Cherry (London, Academic Press Inc., 1955), p. 227.
10. John Von Neumann, "The General and Logical Theory of Automata," in *The World of Mathematics*, vol. 4, p. 209.

7: DEFENSE SYSTEMS

1. O. H. Schmitt, "The Design of Machines to Simulate the Behavior of the Human Brain," in *IRE National Convention, 1955, Symposium,* pp. 240–55.
2. *Business Week* (June 21, 1958), pp. 68–92.
3. *Time* (December 8, 1958), vol. 72, No. 22, p. 73.
4. *The New Yorker* (December 6, 1958), pp. 44–45.
5. J. T. Culbertson, "Some Uneconomical Robots," in *Automata Studies,* ed. by C. E. Shannon and J. McCarthy (Princeton University Press, 1956), p. 110.
6. ". . . the logical approach and structure in natural automata may be expected to differ widely from those in artificial automata." John Von Neumann, *The Computer and the Brain* (New Haven, Yale University Press, 1958), p. 52.
7. Richard Bellman, "On 'Heuristic Problem Solving' by Simon and Newell," in *Operations Research* (May–June, 1958), Vol. 6, No. 3. Bellman's note is important enough and fortunately short enough to present in full:

"For those who are interested in becoming prophets with honor in their own time and in their own country, there is a fundamental principle which we may call the PRINCIPLE OF OPTIMISM: *Never make negative predictions.*

"All of us . . . recall with glee the predictions of outstanding authorities who stated the impossibility of air travel, the lack of utility of Hertzian waves, the impossibility of rocket engines, and so forth. But who pays attention to the hundreds of outpourings of over-enthusiasm that never materialize? One valid prediction completely outshadows the hundred wild ones, since Nostradamus is never judged percentage-wise.

"On page 7 of the article by Simon and Newell, four predictions are made concerning the usage of computers within ten years, predictions concerning the discovery of important mathematical theorems, the writing of worthwhile music, the future dependence of the major part of the field of psychology upon computers, and the dethroning of the current world chess champion by a computer.

8: Meaning as a Continuum

"It would be courageous to make any one of these statements, particularly with a short time like ten years attached. It is magnificent to make all four—and several others sprinkled through Simon and Newell's text. It is magnificent, but it is not scientific writing.

"I feel that to use terms like 'that think, that learn, and that create,' without a careful statement as to what is meant by these terms in connection with machines is irresponsible. This careless usage merely adds to the mysticism that surrounds problem areas difficult enough by any standards.

"These topics are too important to be obscured in this way and too important to be sensationalized in this fashion. Anyone who has examined the formidable difficulties in the statement of criteria, and the prescription of policies, much less the programming of machines to accomplish some of these tasks, will deplore statements of this type."

8. For an extended discussion of this topic, see Chapter 8.

9. Cornell Aeronautical Laboratory, *The Perceptron: A Theory of Statistical Separability in Cognitive Systems,* prepared by Frank Rosenblatt (January, 1958), Contract No. NONR 2381 (00).

10. Sir C. Sherrington, *The Integrative Action of the Nervous System* (New Haven, Yale University Press, 1906), Second Edition, Third Printing, 1952, p. 380.

11. Sir C. Sherrington, *Man on His Nature* (Cambridge, Cambridge University Press, 1953), pp. 213–14.

12. F. Rosenblatt, "The Design of an Intelligent Automaton," in *Research Reviews* (Washington, Office of Naval Research, October, 1958), p. 6.

13. J. C. Eccles, *The Neurophysical Basis of Mind* (Oxford, Clarendon Press, 1956), pp. 261–86.

8: MEANING AS A CONTINUUM

1. W. V. O. Quine, "The Problem of Meaning in Linguistics," in *From a Logical Point of View* (Cambridge, Harvard University Press), 1953, p. 48.

2. Alfred Tarski, *Logic, Semantics, Metamathematics* (Oxford, Clarendon Press, 1956), p. 406.

3. Ibid., p. 156.

ADDENDUM

1. John Carter and Graham Pollard, *An Enquiry into the Nature of Certain Nineteenth Century Pamphlets* (London, Constable and Co., Ltd., 1934), p. 94.

Bei Fragen zur Produktsicherheit wenden Sie sich bitte an:
If you have any questions regarding product safety,
please contact:

Walter de Gruyter GmbH
Genthiner Straße 13
10785 Berlin
productsafety@degruyterbrill.com